LUST

and

Its Posse

A Workbook to Deliverance

ILAYA BROWN

ISBN: 9781670518286

DEDICATION

To my loveliest Phebe! If you ever need this workbook, I pray that it allows you the ultimate freedom it brought to me. I love that you and I are growing together and learning ourselves in the process. Anyta Hall, thank you for your patience, understanding, and ability to be a spiritual mother who could speak life into me. Kathleen and Roger Delaney, thanks for allowing my wild choices to be my growing pains. Best parents a girl could ask for. I love you all!

CONTENTS

Dedication iii
Contents v
Acknowledgments i
Introduction 1
Work 1: Lust of The Eyes 5
Work 2: Ears; your hearing 10
Work 3: Smell 15
Work 4: Taste 21
Work 5: Touch 26
Praise Break! 34
Part Two 36
Introduction to part two 37
Spiritual Warfare 39
Experience 1: Tempted 47
Experience 2: Insomnia 51
Experience 3: Rejection 56
Experience 4: Regret 61
Experience 5: Bitterness 68
Experience 6: Low Self-Esteem 74
Experience 7: Sensuality 81
Experience 8: Sexual Immorality 86
Experience 9: Pride 92
Experience 10: Lack of Natural Affection 97
Experience 11: Addictions 101
Afterword 106
About the Author 108

ACKNOWLEDGMENTS

Jah! Jehovah! My Lord Jesus the Christ! Precious Holy Spirit! Thank You for seeing more in me than I could ever imagine of myself. Thank You for trusting me to be obedient to complete the work. I am ever in awe of You. To You be the Glory!

INTRODUCTION

A steamy scene from a movie; that short skirt that passed you on the street; those broad shoulders that made eye contact with you; those pearly whites flashing… any or all of them could have your groin aching with desire. Lust presents itself in an instance. It's up to you to rebuke it with the Word of God. Not even that deep prayer stuff. Just say 'Jesus' and walk off or say 'No!' and think of something positive.

The truth is that the root is already there. The gates to the soul are the eyes. There are other entry points such as the ears (hearing), sense of smell, taste, and touch that can activate what is deep inside our inner self. We discuss the eyes first because they are usually the initial point of contact; the others follow. Contact must happen before the other senses, or gates, can have effect. We will look at how these gates can be an entry point of the enemy – the enemy in this case being your own mind and the devil.

This book is a safe place to be open about the wounds and weaknesses that will have one succumbing to their own lusts and feeling enticed (Jas. 1:14). This book is in workbook format because we must allow the Holy Spirit to bring things up to our remembrance so we can repent, confess, and turn from that behavior. Have a notebook ready because suppressed memories that have been forgotten can be devastating when recollected. We will be using mainly the scriptures from the King James Version of the Bible, unless I state otherwise. I chose this version because I find that its poetic nature makes it quite impactful. I suggest that for the scripture references I plug in, you read the verses before and after the reference so you can get the fullness of the text. Scripture is best understood in context.

It is great to have a spiritual leader — someone who's trustworthy in this process — to help you overcome. A foundational church home is ideal as well. A church of deliverance is even better. When you're dealing with things of the soul it is imperative not to forsake the assembly with others. It is a strengthening mechanism for the soul (Heb. 10:25).

Deliverance is a fight. You must want it, and you must ask for it from the Lord Jesus. It's a fight to get it and a fight to keep it. God gives it to us freely but the enemy, the devil, wants to keep us bound with lies and deceit. If he has accusations, he will bring them up to keep a person in bondage. The devil comes to steal, kill, and destroy, but Jesus is alive so that we may have life and have it more abundantly right now (John 10:10). That's why it is important to confess your weaknesses to the heavenly Father to get free (John 8:31-36).

Now, everything I'm going to share in this book hinges on you being saved. Random people won't just take up this book, say a few prayers, write a few lines, and get delivered. No. You've got to be in a right relationship with Jesus Christ for *any* of this to be applicable to your life.

It's your choice or not to get saved, and don't try to pretend you're saved just to get what this book offers. But if you are at a place where you're truly ready to accept Jesus Christ into your heart; believe He died for your sins, and confess with your mouth that He is Lord, then I encourage you to pray this prayer with me right now. We will also put our journey to deliverance before the Lord:

> I accept Jesus Christ as my Lord and Savior. I believe He died on the cross for me and rose again and lives with all power as the Living Son of God.
>
> Most Holy Father, Lamb of God, and activating Holy Spirit, I pray that reading and working this book will free me once the prayers and tools of this book are applied. I pray You, God, will deal with all personally. I pray that I will receive deliverance and that I will be a testimony for others. I bind any pseudo-memories that will try to take over my mind.

> I thank You, God, that in this process I will not be made ashamed. I curse any retaliating forces and bind them in Jesus' name! Amen!

Praying this prayer, and doing do sincerely, if you were not walking with the Lord before, you have now received salvation and the angels in heaven are rejoicing at your return to God. Hallelujah!!! Now, you have access to the many benefits, some of which you will find between the covers of this book.

WORK 1: LUST OF THE EYES

Traditional chapter headings are not what this book is about. This workbook is just that: *work*. It is broken up into sections that you can easily follow and reference if you need a refresher.

We can start with my personal testimony. I was a preteen. It was summer and my brother and I were latch-key kids. We had a lot of unsupervised time on our hands. One day, a child from the neighborhood brought over a video home system tape, or VHS, of pornography. Do you remember those, the VHS tapes?

Of course, we all watched it out of curiosity. For those who have not watched pornography, consider yourself blessed. Pornography is very explicit and gets up close and personal, showing how God intended for us to procreate. The difference is those in the video are not married and a lot of times there are more than two partners. Furthermore, it is an unrealistic form of intimacy, and is very deceiving because it is not how God intended for us to join in holy matrimony and know our partner.

One cannot un-see what has been seen. That seed was planted and started a rabbit hole of desires I shouldn't have had as a child, and certainly not before the age of 12! Truth be told, a few years ago a suppressed memory came up of where my first kiss came from. I was six or seven and the neighbors down the street were boy and girl, just like my brother and me. The little girl was older than me. She gave me my first kiss. You think nothing of it. You're a child and feel safe because it's another child. I watched kissing scenes in movies (again with the eye gates) and I didn't see harm in it. Again, I was only six.

I later found out from a parent that those children were exposed to pornography via their father's stash and it caused a ruckus between our families. They moved after that and I didn't see that girl until we were both grown women. At that time, I had been saved a few years and I just couldn't understand why seeing her made me extremely angry, even though she was happy to see me. I didn't know the details regarding why they had moved and our families getting into a dispute. God showed me when I was praying on the matter and revealed what I had forgotten.

God informed me that homosexuality, which is a spirit, had been after me a long time. He revealed to me that the Holy Spirit within me identified a spirit that was not His own in her and that natural reaction in me was anger. I was so uneasy after prayer. Thank God for His precious Holy Ghost and Jesus, the sacrifice!

We will discuss the supernatural side of reality. It is very much reality in that what manifests in what we see with our natural eyes has already manifested in the unseen. If you have faith, then it's not hard for you to grasp the concept of the unseen world that runs parallel to this one.

Back to the beginning! I started watching that first video alone. I would watch adult channels on cable when everyone was asleep. I would listen to seductive music and masturbate. My favorite artist to listen to is the one who is now in the media in Chicago and Atlanta for alleged sex crimes with underage girls. Music is a powerful tool to activate inner lusts and desires because music can carry certain spirits. The things that were allegedly going on in the studio while these songs were being recorded activated certain spirits and I believe listening to that music allowed those spirits to be transferred to me.

There are some worship songs that can take you high into the spirit and have you feeling like you're in God's bosom. There are other praise and worship songs that will have you forgetting they are talking about Jesus because they activate your memories of being in the club. Be careful of what you allow to enter your ears. We'll be going there next.

After a while, watching porn was the only way I could get to sleep. Looking back at that situation, I can say that it was terrible. There I

was, a child needing more than a binky to get to bed. I couldn't tell anyone. I had to keep it a secret. I thought my family would look at me
strange and I was ashamed. Then I would ask myself, *How can you be ashamed if you really don't know what you're doing, and why?*

I tell my mentees if you must do something in secret then chances are it's wrong. Your mind is equipped with a wrongdoing radar — whether it's lessons learned from a parent or life choices you have seen others make — you know when something is out of pocket and you're convicted.

I know God has me telling all my business, but it's to help others. We will say a prayer and allow the Holy Spirit to deal with you on the matter of your beginning. These pages are your secret place with the Maker. This prayer is what I call the "Snatch the Drawers Off Prayer." God had me in the book of Jeremiah for a time and when I came across chapter 13, it changed my life. I started putting people's names in while reading the scripture. It was powerful to see how people would openly confess things to me. I would tell my girlfriends how to pray the prayer and they would be either happy or devastated when they realized the true intentions of people. "Why are we praying this over ourselves?" you may ask. Because our hearts are deceitful and can be wicked in nature, so it takes the Word of God to reveal our true selves and buried secrets (Jer. 17:9).

When things come up, confess them. Speak your confession into the atmosphere. Cry out unto God and release it to Him. Some things will be hard to say, but that's okay. Ask God for strength to get deliverance. Be open to letting go of what separates you from Christ and a personal relationship with God. If you picked up this book and read the introduction and continued reading, you wanted this change. Accept it so you can grow and move forward.

Once you have confessed all that you have seen in your mind's eye concerning memories and past sins, plea the blood of Jesus Christ over it. Saying, "I plea the blood of Jesus over it" covers it and it can't be brought up once released and covered. Remember, you can't uncover it either! Close prayer by saying "in the name of Jesus" and continue forward in the work.

If you have your heavenly language it is good if you pray in the Spirit after reading the prayers. If you don't, then I recommend praying for your heavenly* *language until you get it, and in the meantime, call on the name of Jesus and pray the scripture (I recommend the Psalms).

Prayer

Jehovah, we ask why these things come upon us. We ask for You to give us knowledge and wisdom on where the seed that caused our perversion was planted. We ask that You discover our skirts upon our faces so that our shame will be made bare (Jer. 13:26). We ask that if our perversion was caused by another person, You give us the root cause so we can pray effectively. God, we pray that with the enlightening of our eyes You give us strength to face the truth and that with this truth You will make us free. In the name of Jesus! Amen.

WORK 2: EARS; YOUR HEARING

"Do you hear what I hear?" The telephone game is a wonderful tool that shows how people can miscommunicate the simplest phrase or instruction. The first person in an assembled line receives a whispered phrase and they must tell the next person. The next person shares it with the next and the process continues. Once it gets to the person at the end of the line, the phrase is generally nothing like what was initially communicated.

Allowing things into our ear gates allows positivity or negativity to come in. If you listen to music that has explicit lyrics about violence or sexual content, it will heighten those senses within you. If you listen to that person who tells you that you will never amount to anything, your self-esteem is diminished.

You have full control over what you listen to music-wise. It is hard to get away from a person who isn't feeding you in a good way spiritually if they are a spouse, parent, or guardian. Those wounds will have you seeking comfort in the arms of other people or getting a temporary fix by self-medicating with drugs, masturbation, or sex.

When a person does not feel they are enough in one sense, they will try to prove they are in other ways. Some people join gangs; resort to violence; use material things to gain others' affections; use their bodies to get a sense of love.

Hosea 4:1 says, "Hear the word of the Lord, ye children of Israel: for the Lord hath a controversy with the inhabitants of the land, because there is no truth, nor mercy, nor knowledge of God in the land."

The things we choose to partake in are just that – a choice. We choose our friends, the music we listen to, the things we read, and the places we visit. We turn away from God when we make the choice not to read the Word, go to church, or even govern ourselves with the Truth of the Gospel because we reject it when we don't pick up the book or make our best attempt to live what's stated in the pages.

This example I'm going to give is a bit radical, but it will make the point. Jesus comes in and sees a ton of foolishness going on in His temple. There are people consuming alcohol, gambling, having an orgy, committing adultery, lying, stealing, being violent, and displaying unnatural affection through homosexuality. He gets angry and turns over tables and drives out the things that cause us to err (John 2:15). Because we don't know who we are in Christ — that WE are the CHURCH — we in turn put Jesus out by rejecting Him in our hearts. We quench the Holy Spirit that convicts us of our evil ways and continue to satisfy our flesh. We continue to listen to those things that do not edify us. Continuing in the same behavior, we go back to the thing that we initially saw with our eyes and again begin to desire those things. We once again start doing that same thing we were delivered from, all because we heard a song that sparked a memory, or there was something said in innocent conversation that brought something to our recollection and put that picture to the forefront of our mind's eye. Now we want it again!

It's a cycle. Truth be told, it wasn't that good! The crazy thing about how the devil works is that he will make that memory seem so fantastic that you forget the disrespect that happened before or after those enjoyable few minutes. Yes, once you get back in it, you realize it only happened for a few minutes; you still weren't satisfied, and you're now in a worse condition than before.

Matthew 12:43-45 is Jesus explaining how keeping a clean house is parallel to our mental state and condition of our soul. The Christian Standard Bible translates it thus:

> When an unclean spirit comes out of a person, it roams through waterless places looking for rest but doesn't find any. Then it says, 'I'll go back to my house that I came from.' Returning, it finds the house vacant, swept, and put in order. Then it goes and brings with it seven other spirits more evil

> than itself, and they enter and settle down there. As a result, that person's last condition is worse than the first. That's how it will also be with this evil generation.

We must be careful what we allow in our church, our bodies, our minds! We are the church, according to 1 Corinthians 3:16-17, which basically says, "Don't you yourselves know that you are God's temple and that the Spirit of God lives in you? If anyone destroys God's temple, God will destroy him; for God's temple is holy, and that is what you are." (NIV)

We have been informed of whose we are and what we are. Now is the occasion of prayer. It can be a very drastic thing to ask for you to stop listening to secular music and put away those friends that speak death over you and not life BUT you have to choose your soul and salvation at all cost. Eternity is a long, long time!

If you are a young adult and it's a parent who is speaking those things over you, then you must allow the light of Christ to shine from within you. The evil in that person will see your light and it will inspire change, hopefully. In my case, I wanted to live in sin without shame. When I got of legal age and moved out, I received the call of salvation at age 19. I had all other intentions, but God had other plans!

You must read the Word of God daily. Read your Bible every day. I used to read 10 chapters a day: five Psalms and five from other books in the Word. How else do you think I made it through 10 years of celibacy? It wasn't until I grew weary and backslid that the crap hit the fan. Let us prepare for prayer. Roman's chapter seven is where God is leading, so that's where were the foundation scripture will be.

PRAYER

Father, in the name of Jesus, we come to You asking for a zeal to serve You. We ask that You put us in the correct places, around the right people, and in our right mind. We acknowledge the evil within us is ever present. We acknowledge that in our flesh dwelleth no good thing. We know good but evil is what we do. Clean us up, Holy Father, in the name of Jesus. Help us to delight in Your law after the inward man: there is the world of sin that is warring within us to stomp out the good You have called us into. Teach us to pray as we should, for we know not how to pray. Train our hearing to turn to things that are above in Your Holy Place and tune out the things of this world. Change our surrounding and convert our hearts to Christ. This prayer we pray in Jesus' name. Amen.

WORK 3: SMELL

Certain perfumes can have one back in their mother's kitchen after she has cooked Sunday dinner; in the club grinding on that fine fella you had a one-night stand with, or feeling like a child who was taken advantage of. Smell has such a strong connection to memories it is amazing. My mother worked at the hospital for years and has since retired. I don't know if it's the hospital soap they use, but every time I enter the building or get a sniff of nurses on lunch break, I think of my mother.

There are moments when smelling something is not so pleasant. When you smell a decaying carcass on the side of the road, that's not pleasant; you want to get away from it. I had backslidden for the second time, and God came to me. He informed me that I stunk in His nostrils and let me know I needed to choose.

Yes, I'm a Holy Ghost-filled, blood-washed believer! I am by no means perfect. I do know when God is fed up because I have read enough scripture to know when you start to stink to Him, He can't tolerate you in His presence. We can take it to the Word. This passage is discussing how to make an offering of fragrance to the Lord. When a sacrifice is to be made to God, it is extremely specific. The Bible is particular and concise regarding what ingredients to put it in, who is to offer the sacrifice, and how they are to perform it. There is a perfume in the scripture that must be made for the Lord. There is a warning after the instruction that if a person duplicates the perfume, or "makes one like unto it" they are to be cut off from their people (Exod. 30:38).

Certain spirits have a smell. I backslid in my fornication and rebellion and I'm sure I smelled just like those sins to the Lord. I had to make a choice; I couldn't straddle the fence. I had to be hot or cold because Jesus informed us He would "spue" — that is to say *spit* — you out of His mouth if you're lukewarm (Rev. 3:16).

I know of a person who was sexually molested by a close friend of the family. The abuse lasted for years. As an adult, they could not tolerate the smell of Old Spice; they would physically become ill. Even years after this person was removed from the situation, no matter where we were, if that scent hit their nose, they were out of there, or felt like they were about to throw up. That is the level of control a situation can have on a person; not to mention how common the scent of that particular product is because it's affordable. You must bend your life around not encountering what has hurt you or has you bound, so you can't reflect on the memory of a situation. Jesus wants to make you free of that very thing that would have you quivering in fear!

We are going to pray that the fragrance of trauma be removed from the nostrils. We're going to pray that the very smell that activates lustful desires be broken from the necks of the oppressed in the name of Jesus!

Deception can come with an odor or smell. Jacob was able to fool his father Isaac by pretending he was his brother Esau. He was able to do it because Isaac was old and had no eyesight. Jacob put on Esau's clothes and put fur on himself (because his brother was a hairy man). Jacob wanted the blessing that was due to the firstborn. He received it because Isaac figured he had the correct son. Isaac says, "See, the smell of my son is as the smell of a field which the Lord hath blessed." (Gen. 27:27b)

The deception of smell can you have in utter confusion. When it comes to unnatural affection, women can smell themselves and figure that's the only scent they're to gravitate to; likewise for men. Confusion can start at an early age. We try to make a situation so complex but when you're reading the Word of God things can be made plain to you. Confusion will even have you justifying a situation by misinterpreting the Word of God so that your heart can feel less pricked with the truth.

A great example would be the Tower of Babel. Genesis 11:1-9

goes into detail about how the Lord confounded the language of the people so they could not build a tower that reached the heavens. *Webster's Dictionary* explains *confound* to mean *confusion.* Stating it this way makes it seem like God created confusion. It's stated in scripture that God is not the author of confusion, but of peace (1 Cor. 14:33). What God did was mix up their language and thereby scatter the people to different parts of the earth. *Mix up* is another translation for *confound*, same dictionary.

"Why would God do a thing like that?" you may ask. Do you remember the devil? He was in charge of the praise and worship of God; a top-ranked angel who got puffed up in pride and ended up being kicked out of heaven. It wasn't just Lucifer who was kicked out, but every other angel he was able to convert to worship him was kicked out as well. Think of it! If man was able to build a tower that reached to the throne of God, do you think man would feel they needed God for anything? We would be in the same state as the devil: defeated and looking for others to go to hell in the same caravan because that too would be the destiny of those who do not keep God as their source. Don't mix up confusion with grace in this example. Hallelujah!

Confusion caused by what scents are attractive to you can cause a person to chase unnatural affection. It can be a comforting mechanism or attachment to trauma that causes a person to seek the selfsame desires. Specifically, I'm talking about someone seeking comfort in the arms of someone who smells like them, because someone who smelled like the opposite sex caused them trauma. This can lead to same-sex desires, but in reality, our desire should be to please the Lord and to maintain a relationship with Jesus the Christ.

> Now thanks be unto God, which always causeth us to triumph in Christ, and maketh manifest the savour of his knowledge by us in every place. For we are unto God a sweet savour of Christ, in them that are saved, and in them that perish: To the one we are the savour of death unto death; and to the other the savour of life unto life. And who is sufficient for these things? (2 Cor 2:14-16)

Your smell — savor — can trigger a memory, creating desires that are attached to things you have heard, which bring up the picture show that is your memory bank. That's why it is important to get to the root of the issue in order for you not to be deceived and carried off into ignorance without an understanding of why you feel bound and certain triggers can have you a nonfunctioning person in the real world.

These simple, yet complex, things can have you masturbating in the bathroom on your lunchbreak just like me! Deliverance is powerful and the process to get it can be draining in the moment, but pressing forward and reaping the reward of freedom from the shame, guilt, and regret of those secret (or open) sins will have you in a better state of consciousness and open to receive the many blessings God has for you in Jesus' name!

If after these examples and explanation, you don't feel smell is powerful, I dare you to think of a time someone has passed you with some good-smelling food. Didn't you look in the direction from which the smell was coming? I bet you knew exactly what food it was and if you're chunky like me, you might know what restaurant serves it. Same thing! The smell of a thing can have the hairs on your neck stand up in fear, you breaking out in tears, or your members pulsating in stimulation. Let us pray!

Prayer

Heavenly Father, You have brought us this far. You said You would never leave us nor forsake us. We come to You with open minds, open hearts, and open mouths begging for forgiveness. God, transform us. Let this mind be in us that is also in Christ Jesus. We bind our mind to the Mind of Christ. We are tempted when we are drawn away by our own lusts and we feel enticed. We pray the door to our lustful desires that come by way of smell, hearing, and the eye gates be closed in the name of Jesus. We pray that with this confession, You reveal Yourself to us; reveal our weak areas. God, You said in Your Word that You create a way of escape in the time of temptation. Place a hedge of protection around our minds in Jesus' name just as Job was hedged in. God, we pray with today's revelation comes swift deliverance. It's in Your Son Jesus' name we pray. Amen!

WORK 4: TASTE

Life and death are in the power of the tongue (Prov. 18:21). Just as this small member contains the power of life, it can be a triggering source for lustful desires. Taste is something that involves the nose and the entire tongue to really savor what you're eating. One can tell exactly what they're eating if they are blindfolded, or one can tell a dish is missing a specific spice.

Raspberry lip gloss, lotion on the skin, or body fluids can entice lustful desires that will have you craving the person or thing in order to satisfy the temptation. It's like unto an addiction. Once you get hot on the scent, like a hound you must have it. Paul says it better, "Meats for the belly, and the belly for meats: but God shall destroy both it and them. Now the body is not for fornication, but for the Lord; and the Lord for the body." (1 Cor. 6:13)

I received the call of salvation at the age of 19. I took a vow of celibacy then and kept it until I was 29. I did not have intercourse. Weariness in waiting caused my backsliding. I found someone I was spending a ton of time with and we justified using our mouths for pleasure. Once that began to occur, we wanted more, naturally! That led to a quick marriage that was outside of God's will for my life. I have a beautiful daughter from that marriage, but it was to a person who didn't believe in Jesus, and I was backslidden and didn't consult God at all before I got married.

Once you open the door to let in a little sin, it won't be long before you dive right in and go all the way. Tasting the fluids of another person whether by kissing or oral sex creates a soul tie.

You're swapping one another's juices and digesting them. It's becoming a part of your body just as if it were meat or water. Who's to say what your body will accept and reject for nutrients?

Now that you have opened the door to taste, it won't be long before those desires cloud your thoughts and make it hard to focus. It will be all you can think of! It's hard to have a holy life when your mind is working against you in overtime. Not to mention, once you take that little step toward fulfilling your fleshly lust the enemy will come in and whisper, "You might as well have sex. Didn't you climax with them already? Going all the way won't hurt!"

In my decade of celibacy, I did a lot of saying "Jesus" when thoughts would come across my mind. It was helpful the person I desired the most was over 200 miles away and I didn't have transportation. There were times of yearning when all I wanted was his lips after we kissed. A fool would think I wasn't wondering what the rest of the package was like. I sure was! There was a time we came close too, but it just didn't happen for whatever reason. In hindsight I'm glad it didn't, because he wasn't supposed to be a permanent fixture in my life. If we would have kept at it, he very well would have been.

We're to taste and see that the Lord is good (Psa. 34:8), even while we await the mate He has called us to be with. Yet we still have a sense of "hold up!" in our members that will not allow total deliverance, which would in turn allow us to focus on God while we wait. When Job was in his trial, to get a closer relationship with God he made reference to putting his tongue to something that wasn't Godly. Job says, "Return, I pray you, let it not be iniquity; yea, return again, my righteousness is in it. Is there iniquity in my tongue? cannot my taste discern perverse things?" (Job 6:29-30)?

The truth is, we get that gut feeling before we do wrong. Before someone presses play on the device that opens your eye gates to a world of fornication; when you open your door or window to see someone in the act and don't turn away; when you overhear some intimate conversations and sounds that imply the very act is happening; catching a certain scent that entices the loins, and tasting a person before the fulfilled time of God can have you in a whirlwind of lust. Lust can separate you from Christ in that it will have you rejecting the very being that is keeping you alive.

A person can get so wrapped up in the physical needs that they don't take notice of the decay of the soul. The soul is eternal and that is what Christ came to save! He came to give us power over the demons and principalities that easily have us turning back to sin instead of pressing in His direction. We must get a hold of our members so that we will not reject Christ. He will never reject us. We are the ones who do the walking away, backsliding, and denying. His arms are never tired of being open wide to receive us when we repent.

We are going to pray that the taste of the world be removed from our mouths. We are going to pray that our mouth be a vessel of praise and that it edifies Christ. Let's surrender the taste we have for the lust of the flesh and desperately seek the perfect will of God. Amen!

Prayer

Heavenly Father, we thank You for the understanding You have allowed us to have, and we stand in full power, knowing that we can't be overtaken by anything that is higher or bigger than what we can bear. God, You are Alpha and Omega and You know the struggle we have in our flesh. We thank You, for the weapons of our warfare are not carnal and You teach us to recognize the ways of escape so that when we are tempted, we can escape. Father, we ask for deliverance and healing and for the very taste of our lustful desires to be removed far from us in the mighty name of Jesus Christ. We renounce the power of Satan over our taste buds. We revoke the privilege we have given the enemy to prevail in our gates. In the name of Jesus. Amen!

WORK 5: TOUCH

Things happen when there is skin-to-skin contact, or even just a simple touch. Our largest organ, the skin, goes into overdrive and all other senses are heightened with a touch. When my daughter was first born, they laid her on my bare chest first thing so that she could feel my warmth and get to know me. She knew my smell, the rhythm of my breathing, my heartbeat, and the sound of my voice before she was born, but that direct contact took our bond to a whole new level. When we touched, a connection was made that went deeper than the womb.

In scripture it says, "Lay hands suddenly on no man, neither be partaker of other men's sins: keep thyself pure." (1 Tim. 5:22) It is important for there to be purity and for you to be set apart, but when scriptures are grouped together, you must pay attention to the full text. Context matters. Before this scripture, Paul discusses how we must rebuke people before everyone so that they may fear the shame of open ridicule and not err because they don't want to be made a public spectacle. Following the referenced scripture, he gives wisdom on how to settle an upset stomach with wine.

Paul touched on transferring spirits with the laying on of hands, but what we're discussing is activating lust. When lust is blown to its full capacity it is sin (Jas. 1:15). We are taught by society and even the media that it is normal to touch ourselves for pleasure and to release our pent-up sexual tension. Men, especially, are taught that the rite of passage is to lose their virginity. For them, that's the process to become a man. They're praised for having multiple partners while a woman is shamed to scorn for doing the same thing.

When we look at the act of touching ourselves, we are really participating in the unnatural use of what is meant for man and woman with our bodies. If you are a man or woman and you're pleasing yourself, wouldn't that be considered man on man, or woman on woman? We must exercise self-control. The Word of the Lord says, "And every man that striveth for the mastery is temperate in all things. Now they do it to obtain a corruptible crown; but we an incorruptible." (1 Cor. 9:25) Where we feel we have no control, Jesus died so that we may strive in the same power He possessed. God had an understanding that the Ten Commandments weren't going to save our souls since we were born into death, but it is the blood of Jesus and the Holy Ghost that show us the way to redemption and everlasting life.

There was a person I knew who was in a relationship. They were engaging in fornication and not keeping themselves for marriage. The women could not "finish" without masturbating before, during, and after sex in order to receive full pleasure. It wasn't that she wasn't attracted to him; she was simply accustomed to this sexual practice. It was at the point where even if she achieved an orgasm, she still needed to please herself almost immediately afterwards. That was damaging to their relationship and it didn't last.

Some are this way with sex toys. Sexual toys that help stimulate certain areas simultaneously or that can be used without a person present is just like pornography. It gives a false sense of intimacy. It's unrealistic in that because you're receiving orgasmic pleasure, you're unaware that you're missing out on knowing your partner, which is a critical aspect of sex within the context of marriage. It's up to you both to find those spots and lead each other to ecstasy – that's the part of knowing your partner the way God intended. This knowing is what binds you as one flesh. It's why sex seals the deal when it comes to marriage. Even though the American court system is somewhat accepting towards things that are ungodly, they still ask when you wish to annul a marriage if it was consummated. They have an understanding that the marriage was official once the couple has had sex as husband and wife. Deep, I know!

When it comes to toys, we must understand that no man or women can vibrate or make muscles pulsate in the same way that a machine can. It's not realistic! Some may not see any wrong in this portion of the text and that's up to you. We're discussing what is biblically sound. I haven't seen a scripture yet that discusses a marriage or a sexual act that includes taking another item into the bedroom in the scripture. In scripture to 'know' someone was to say they had sex (Gen 4:1, 4:17, 4:25).

Masturbation and sex toys have us rolling to the next point: INTERCOURSE!!! Sorry, I felt the need to sing it.

I'm not a virgin. I didn't hold myself for marriage. After my divorce, I didn't hold myself for marriage either. Once that flood gate has been reopened, it's so hard to close it. I've made strides and asked God for deliverance in order to get to the marriage of my destiny. It's hot, y'all, but hell is real and even hotter. Disclaimer out of the way, here we go!

Intercourse is such a deposit in God's bank, I can't even tell you. When you go through the book of Genesis, in the first few chapters of man and woman before the fall, you don't see marriage mentioned. They were tending to the garden. It wasn't until after they both ate the forbidden fruit that God mentions childbirth and that Adam "knew" Eve. What were they doing in the meantime? Working and being busy. They had no knowledge of nakedness. That's why I stayed busy in my years of celibacy so that I wouldn't recognize my nakedness. It worked for a long time.

Sex between two people serves to tie them into a covenant with God and to establish a blood line of offspring. The sex is to be between male and female. It is only through intercourse between male and female that they can conceive and reproduce. I don't care how you scientifically get it done, you need *his* seed to fertilize *her* egg to make it grow.

God designed our bodies to make sex interesting. He wouldn't have made such an act so pleasurable if He didn't want you to have fun doing it. We are naturally curious creatures. What better positions in which to place stimulating areas of the body than spots where you would have to explore to find them? The marital bed between a husband and wife is undefiled (Heb. 13:4); they can't mess it up unless they bring in another person or idol.

You may be asking me, "What do you mean 'the marital bed is undefiled'? Does that mean my spouse and I can agree to have a threesome?" The scripture reads, "Marriage is honourable in all, and the bed undefiled: but whoremongers and adulterers God will judge."

(Heb. 13:4) God is particular in His instruction because His goal is to be preventative. God doesn't want you to give an opportunity for you two to be separated. That's why Jesus was the ultimate sacrifice, and the Holy Ghost is a gift to keep you on the straight and narrow path back to the Heavenly Father.

There are only two sins that you commit that could prevent you from returning to God. One is to blaspheme against the Holy Ghost (Matt. 12:31). It is fitting, because to blaspheme the Holy Ghost is to rebuke the very air you breathe, your way of existence, and even the way your generations were put into action because the Holy Spirit is the action of God. You curse that or speak death over it, you speak death to your generations going forward.

The second one is unforgiveness. The scripture reads, "For if ye forgive men their trespasses, your heavenly Father will also forgive you: but if ye forgive nor men their trespasses, neither will your Father forgive your trespasses." (Matt. 6:14-15)

Forgiveness is a heavy weight. Some of you reading this book may not have gotten into your lustful situation willingly. Rape is a spirit that manifests in molestation, abortion, rejection, bitterness, addiction, sensuality, and sexual impurity. Rape is a robbery of the body in the supernatural. It takes away a person's choice in what they will do with their own bodies. It also puts the victim in a place where they must forgive. Unforgiveness can block a person from growth and the life God wishes for them to have and that includes the eternal afterlife. The deliverance must be done internally. The Goddess Pearls — those vaginal detox beads that you insert for "cleansing" — that are being touted right now can't rid you of past lovers, things of the past, and bad decisions. Only God can do that.

That was heavy but stay with me. When you have intercourse outside of marriage, that is fornication. Fornication is the sexual act of two people who are not married. You can fornicate with anything – someone of the same sex; self-sex; someone of the opposite sex, or toys that cause a climax. Even bestiality comes into play! Men would lie with sheep and goats because the female innards felt like a women's (so I heard here in the Deep South). People of both sexes have been known to place different foods on their body so their favorite pet would lick it off. Like a man, a woman can lie with animals as well. That is not of God.

When you lie with someone a deposit is made. You're locked

together. You're hitched! Hence the old phrase 'We're hitched' when a couple get married. You're now joined together and are attached. Fornication is a hitch that happens without a covenant and isn't a blessing of God. If a child was produced from it, the child is a blessing, but the act to get them here isn't ordained because it was outside of the tie that connects the couple to God.

The unfortunate part about being hitched to someone you have a one-night stand with is that all their demons come with them. You may not know them that well but the demons they carry got acquainted with the demons you haven't been delivered from and some of them stayed to hang with the posse you already had in your members. Psalm 51:7 says, "Purge me with hyssop, and I shall be clean: wash me, and I shall be whiter than snow." When purging has occurred, it is God removing from you those things that do not look like Him or smell like Him, and the condition of your soul that isn't reflecting Him.

When God looks at you, He must see the blood of Jesus, the glory of the Holy Ghost, and His words written on the tablets of your heart. It's a bad day when all He sees are the demons that have attached themselves to you so that you're unrecognizable. Jezebel was the most vicious, hate-filled, murderous, and just pure evil queen in the Bible. This is what God had to say about her:

> Notwithstanding I have a few things against thee, because thou sufferest that woman Jezebel, which calleth herself a prophetess, to teach and to seduce my servants to commit fornication, and to eat things sacrificed unto idols. And I gave her space to repent of her fornication; and she repented not. (Rev. 2:20-21)

Jezebel had the most God-fearing prophet running in fear. If God was sovereign enough to give her the opportunity to get it right, how much more will He do for you? The above is to just point out the two things of which you can't repent in order to get back into a right relationship with God. It's just so you know you have a chance. It's to show you there is hope. You haven't done anything that is too terrible for God.

When you fornicate, you create soul ties. In Jeremiah 3:1, God is asking if a woman is put away from her husband and she gets remarried, and then changes her mind and returns to her first husband, how can she not be polluted? The pollution comes because it's no longer just the first husband's house, but now the wife has the furniture from the second husband and has taken on his ways and conformed to him and has only a few remnants of the first husband. She's changed her hair, gotten tattoos, and now sleeps during the day and stays up all night. She's no longer the same person, but she is still filled with the first husband and now the second husband. Prayerfully, this example comes across clearly.

Soul ties leave you unrecognizable to yourself, and more importantly you're filled with demons, bad habits, and attitudes that were not your own. You must be purged in order to get deliverance from those spirits that have attached to your soul. You've accepted the bond of that person in an act that you felt was a quick fix but has given a lifetime of pain. We are talking way past the fact you became pregnant or got an STD. The STD you contracted was **s**exually **t**ransmitted **d**emons. You can't properly love the child that you got out of the situation because you thought having sex and maybe even a child would lead to marriage or a commitment, but you only got the miracle child out of the deal… of course, this is in addition to the issues that were planted in you during that sexual encounter. You're acting and reacting in ways you normally wouldn't, but since you have those newly attached demons, they're flexing their muscles to see what else they can make you do to get you further and further from God.

When I was purged, I was scared. My tongues changed and became intense. I started spitting up clear liquid, cloudy snot-looking stuff, and blood. The blood scared me, but the Lord informed me that the spirits had become a part of me. They had to come out. There were red markings in my face and neck and arms that looked like my flesh was dotted or ripped under the skin. It frightened me! God took me to the scripture that reads, "And Jesus rebuked him, saying, Hold thy peace, and come out of him. And when the unclean spirit had torn him, and cried with a loud voice, he came out of him." (Mark 1:25-26)

Deliverance is real. Your temple must be wiped clean after engaging in fornication. The Holy Spirit doesn't need to wrestle with what you refuse to give up for you to live your best life on earth and for eternity. The Holy Spirit is a gentleman and will be quenched once you make the choice to operate in knowledgeable unholiness. Once you have come to the truth, you're responsible for the truth you know. You must exercise that truth daily. "For if ye live after the flesh, ye shall die: but if ye through the Spirit do mortify the deeds of the body, ye shall live." (Rom. 8: 13)

Prayer

Father, in the name of Jesus we confess that we have sinned in our bodies and played the harlot with partners and things outside of wedlock. We repent in the name of Jesus. Father, we have laid with beasts as if they were men and women. We repent in the name of Jesus. Father, we have used tools and objects and idolized them for sexual stimulation. God, we have put away the natural use of men and women alike and turned to our own lust. We repent. Lord, we pray for a supernatural manifestation of Your Holy Spirit right now in the name of Jesus. Purge us with hyssop God, wash us and make us whiter than snow. We rebuke the spirit of rape and all spirits that have attached themselves to our soul, heart, mind, and body and cast them to the pits of hell in the name of Jesus! Break every chain and fetter of any soul ties that were created in our lifetime. We call the assignment of the enemy void and aborted in the name of Jesus. We renounce the spirit of Jezebel off our lives and out of our bloodline in the name of Jesus. Father, we bind any devices the adversary wishes to use to come against our minds, our bloodline, our bodies, and our possessions in the name of Jesus. Father, we accept the freedom we are heirs to this day in the name of Jesus. Help us to maintain the freedom and deliverance we received today with Your divine wisdom. In Jesus' name. Amen!

PRAISE BREAK!

The work portion of the book had the purpose of cleaning house. There are things you must do to maintain your deliverance: daily prayer, reading the Word of God, and taking communion consistently.

Communion is the Lord's Supper. This is where Jesus broke bread and shared wine and said, "Take, eat: this is my body which is broken for you.... Take, drink: this is my blood which is shed for you. This do in remembrance of me until I return." (1 Cor. 11:24a-26, paraphrased) Do not take communion if you know you're not living for Jesus and abstaining from sinful ways. A detailed description of what to refrain from is laid out in the book of Romans chapter 8. If you can check the box on any of those, then do not take communion. If you are in unforgiveness against anyone, do not take communion. Get those things right before you partake in the Lord's Holy Communion.

For those who have your heavenly language, pray in it daily. Read the Bible daily. At minimum, read for 15 minutes every day. Everyone has 15 minutes. There are Bible apps you can download on your phone. They still sell the pocket versions of the New Testament that you can carry around. Maintaining your deliverance can be a matter of life and death for some. Take it seriously! Protect it, water your soul and continually seek God so you can know His ways and enhance your understanding of who He is.

If you prayed the prayer of salvation at the beginning of this book, and prayed with meaning and sincerity, you are saved through the blood of Jesus Christ! "That if thou shalt confess with thy mouth the Lord Jesus, and shalt believe in thine heart that God hath raised him from the dead, thou shalt be saved." (Rom. 10:9)

I'm pointing this out because as a child of God and a joint heir with Christ, you can now receive the promise of Jesus. He said:

> And I will pray the Father, and he shall give you another Comforter, that he may abide with you for ever; even the Spirit of truth; whom the world cannot receive, because it seeth him not, neither knoweth him: but ye know him; for he dwelleth with you, and shall be in you. (John 14:16-17)

You have direct access to this promise because you accepted Jesus into your life and heart. I was in the comfort of my own home when I was filled with the Holy Spirit. There is a difference in having the Spirit wooing you. You know that tingle on your skin? That unction to pray or praise God? When you're filled with the Holy Spirit, the evidence of it is speaking in tongues. Acts 2:4 reads, "And they were all filled with the Holy Ghost, and began to speak with other tongues, as the Spirit have them utterance."

I made up in my mind I wanted the promise of God. I was home alone. I put my favorite worship track on repeat and praised God crying "Hallelujah!" until it happened. It wasn't instantaneous for me. I almost gave up, but as soon as I got over my discouragement and started praising God again with a sincere heart, I felt an immeasurable amount of joy and peace. Then it felt like someone was changing my speech. The next thing I knew I was on the floor and my voice changed, my language changed, and I was changed. There hasn't been a greater joy since that day! Nothing compares to that experience.

Praise the Lord for your new freedom, deliverance, and unquenchable fire for Jesus and God and the filling of His Holy Spirit. Take this praise break and do just that: PRAISE!

PART TWO

INTRODUCTION TO PART TWO

The remainder of this book is going to help you know what to look out for while maintaining your deliverance. The enemy will try to come in to destroy what you have worked and asked God for, but you must stand in resistance. God will do the rest! Pray in the spirit if you have your heavenly language. If you haven't yet received that language, then pray the scripture. I recommend the book of Psalms.

> When the unclean spirit is gone out of a man, he walketh through dry places, seeking rest, and findeth none. Then he saith, I will return into my house from whence I came out; and when he is come, he findeth it empty, swept, and garnished. Then goeth he, and taketh with himself seven other spirits more wicked than himself, and they enter in and dwell there: and the last state of that man is worse than the first. Even so shall it be also unto this wicked generation. (Matt. 12:43-45)

We have done some WORK in the first part of this book. That's why the name of each chapter is so fitting. I truly urge you — and your salvation depends on it — to read the Word DAILY. Study the Word of God for yourself. If you depend on someone else to interpret the Word for you, you're fully dependent on what that person thinks is important and what ministers to *them*. I'm not saying you shouldn't listen to others preach and teach the Word; I'm saying you still need to study it for yourself.

If you have your prayer language, even if you received the Holy Spirit with the evidence of speaking in tongues in the praise break earlier in this book, then hallelujah! Pray in the spirit daily! The reason the situation described in the scripture above was so deadly was that the man was empty. The demon can't return with his posse of more wicked spirits than the original if the Holy Spirit can actively manifest in that space and the Word of God has inhabited that space.

I can only tell you what I lived. I made my worst mistakes and had the most drawbacks when I denied Christ, quenched the Holy Spirit, and operated in disobedience. We knowingly throw away the knowledge of God when we don't keep His commandments. Refusing the wisdom He gives us when He instructs us day to day is disobedience. Quenching the Holy Spirit and not allowing Him to operate as He wills leads to sin, damnation, and separation. The Holy Spirit can't dwell in unholiness. Mistakes made in weakness are one thing, but to blatantly disrespect Him and do what you want with the temple of God — your body for which He paid in full by sacrificing His Son — will leave you void, and the Holy Spirit with tape over His mouth. He is a gentleman and will not remain where He is not wanted.

Throw away the knowledge of God and risk missing the basking in His eternal glory, peace, and love? I think not! When we come to ourselves after an error, it is up to us to strive to maintain the correct course on the narrow road to everlasting life. The world allowing things to be the norm doesn't make it right. It REALLY doesn't mean it's right in the eyes of Jehovah.

> (For the weapons of warfare are not carnal, but mighty through God to the pulling down of strong holds;) Casting down imaginations, and every high thing that exalteth itself against the knowledge of God, and bringing into captivity every thought to the obedience of Christ; And having a readiness to revenge all disobedience, when your obedience is fulfilled. (2 Cor. 10:4-6)

The good news is that once you get your house in order you can reach back and at least try to compel to Christ those friends you led astray along the way. We all have left a trail of destruction in our arrogance and life of sin but when you can live by example and pull your homies and family in, then you're fishing for Jesus.

SPIRITUAL WARFARE

Bestiality, pedophilia, homosexuality, and fornication are all sins against your body. A beast or animal may or may not allow the sexual act to take place, but when a spirit of lustful perversion is present the only desire in your flesh is for release. The conscience is seared! You're like the pressure cooker: bubbling over with desire and ready to pounce. The demonic force takes over and has dominion to do so if you're not saved, or you become weak with all the enticing and do the act.

> For though we walk in the flesh, we do not war after the flesh: (For the weapons of warfare are not carnal, but mighty through God to the pulling down of strong holds;) Casting down imaginations, and every high thing that exalteth itself against the knowledge of God, and bringing into captivity every thought to the obedience of Christ; And having a readiness to revenge all disobedience, when your obedience is fulfilled. (2 Cor. 10:3-6)

This scripture is in the introduction to this part of the book, and there is a reason for that. We are going to break it down. There are few people on earth who can see demonic spirits and angels like we see two people sitting down for coffee. The war against good and evil is something that is done in the spirit realm. This war manifests when you see sin full-grown in adultery, fornication, bestiality, pedophilia, murder, strife, homosexuality, and lying – to name a few. The unsaved have no power because they have not accepted Christ as their Lord and savior. When Christ died, He took the keys of death and hell, and He has all power. That same power is given to believers of Christ because it is necessary for our soul's salvation to be able to stand against the various temptations that will happen through life.

This is not to say saved people will have it easy, no. What I'm saying is if there is a war going on and your soul depends on a victory in this fight, it's best to have weapons. The One who holds the keys to the arsenal is Jesus. Accepting Christ snatches you out of the authority of the devil. He can no longer touch you, but he can tempt, or try to persuade you to do evil or sin.

When there are forces that try to tempt you and you can't see them, then you must turn to the Everlasting God who sees all and knows all to prepare you to maintain your salvation. Since you received salvation, your authority through God is to pull down strongholds, reject imaginations that come to your mind, and overcome anything that tries to separate you from the knowledge of God. You have the power to call your mind into obedience of Christ. Your first step in obedience was answering the call of salvation. You became a warrior of God, equipped with what you need. Now, receiving the filling of the Holy Spirit will take you to another level of power! If you received salvation and the Holy Spirit while going through this deliverance manual, God bless you! Keep on pressing! I'm excited with you! Hallelujah!!!

The second part of your obedience is walking in the way the Word instructs. Jesus has full understanding that some things don't change overnight. There are some sins that have been in practice for years. There are some living situations that are firmly rooted, but when the Holy Spirit convicts, it's best you leave in obedience and allow God to take care of you.

When you put away fleshly lust and things that separate you from Christ, you keep yourself out of reach of the devil. He no longer has power over you. He can only make suggestions. He can only suggest that guy or girl is hot and that you should go over and talk to them to see what they're doing later. He can only suggest you see people at a late hour in a mood setting that strikes arousal. It's up to you to resist, take the way of escape Jesus gives, and flee. After all, the Word of God assures us that:

> There hath no temptation taken you but such as is common to man: but God is faithful, who will not suffer you to be tempted above that ye are able; but will with the temptation also make a way to escape, that ye may be able to bear it. (1 Cor. 10:13)

There are experiences that are supernatural that may have gone on before salvation. After getting saved, they may continue to evoke fear. Fear is not a characteristic of God; it's a distraction used by the enemy to come in and entice you into doing a whole deal of things you wouldn't think of.

The incubus "is a nightmare, or the evil spirit that was once supposed to weigh a person down in a nightmare." *(Webster's New World Dictionary 1967)* This evil spirit is also notorious for causing sexual arousal and engaging in sexual intercourse while a person is sleeping. Most of the time ejaculation occurs. It happened to me before I got saved. It started again after I was saved and filled with the Holy Spirit when I began engaging in masturbation and fornication. I opened the door! It is a demonic force that causes you to lose self-control and strikes fear of going to sleep. You can't be on your best game if you're tired from insomnia. We will discuss how a lack of sleep affects you later but know that you're not crazy and those dreams of intense sexual encounters are very real.

If you were molested as a child, or a spirit entered you as a child and now you have a desire to sleep with children, that is the birth of pedophilia. It's a perversion of something God intended to take place only between a married man and his wife. Someone entering a sexual act with flat-out fear isn't the pleasure of what God intended to be the beautiful agreement seal of His covenant with two people. It's robbery and rape!

Let's see where this stuff started. Genesis 6:1-5 reads,

> And it came to pass, when men began to multiply on the face of the earth, and daughters were born unto them, That the sons of God saw the daughters of men that they were fair; and they took them wives of all which they chose. And the Lord said, My spirit shall not always strive with man, for that he also is flesh: yet his days shall be an hundred and

> twenty years. There were giants in the earth in those days; and also after that, when the sons of God came in unto the daughters of men, and they bare children to them, the same became mighty men which were of old, men of renown. And God saw that the wickedness of man was great in the earth, and that every imagination of the thoughts of his heart was only evil continually.

Let's see how this was incorrect in the eyes of God. Jehovah is a God of order. The fathers of these women were giving their daughters away to these fallen angels to be married. Verse four in the NIV version reads, "In those days, and for some time after, giant Nephilies lived on the earth, for whenever the sons of God had intercourse with women they gave birth to children who became the heroes and famous warriors of ancient times." When we see marriage or that a male takes a wife in the text, it separates sons of God from daughters of man as if they were not of the same species. These two procreating created a form of mankind different from everyone else. They would have needed God's permission and blessing to do so. God would have had to consent! Since no such consent appears to have been given, the fathers of the bride operated outside of God's consent. On top of that, the fathers of the bride had full knowledge of who these beings were. They had the knowledge that they were fallen angels and workers of iniquity.

Think about it! In chapter five of Genesis it's reiterated that God created man and women, Adam and Eve, and that He blessed them. The genealogy is laid out from Adam to the existing generation at the time. Turn to the next chapter, chapter six, where the sons of God appear and take "daughters of men" to wife. God says His spirit will not always strive with man and cuts the length of life of man. Man's wickedness grieved God. They had to have a certain look about them if they created giants!

Job chapter one reads, "Now there was a day when the sons of God came to present themselves before the LORD, and Satan also came among them." We see here that the sons of God would go before the Father. The sons of God had to know their limits if they were in direct communication with God. The one human in scripture that was said to have walked with God didn't see death and was taken. That was Enoch (Gen. 5:24). Moses was in the presence of God and his face began to shine (Exo. 34:29-30). Therefore, it's hard to believe the sons of God were before God and didn't receive specific instructions on what they could and could not do. Even Satan received instructions on what he could do to Job.

When we walk outside the will of God, we open the door for Satan to enter and have full authority to do what he wants. That is why it is so important to walk in obedience with God's Word.

Let's take today, for example. You know a person is of the devil if there isn't a relationship to Christ and God in sight. If they are not filled with the Holy Spirit, their conversation will not be of holiness but one of taking. Specifically, their presence can take your joy, peace, and finances. The enemy comes to steal, kill, and destroy (John 10:10)! All you must do is not be in a rush; instead, in all things remain watchful and in prayer. Try the spirit by the spirit to see if it is of God (1 John 4:1) – whether a person's character aligns with the Word of God, the conversation is edifying and not always tearing you down, and they do not try to stand in the way of your relationship with Christ. If it's of God, it will be a mirror image of God. The nine spirits of Christ will be on display continually. These are referred to as the fruit of the spirit. It's because as a believer draws to Christ and their relationship deepens, these characteristics will be on full display. The fruit is as follows: love, joy, peace, longsuffering, gentleness, goodness, faith, meekness, and temperance (Gal 5:22-23.)

"And Asa did that which was right in the eyes of the Lord, as did David his father. And he took away the sodomites out of the land, and removed all the idols that his fathers had made." (1 Kin. 15:11-12) Sodomy goes against the laws of gravity and the instruction of the intestines. Without being too graphic, let me just say that food goes into the mouth and the excess the body doesn't need is passed as feces. Those muscles move internal contents towards the exit, and we're not designed – neither male nor female – for things to enter that place of exit. Sodomy is practiced in male homosexuality and it has to be removed from the equation in order to do what is right in the sight of God. Women can partake in anal sex as well. It's still the same context because the body was not designed in that way. I know it is stated that the marital bed is undefiled; however, there are practices that should have Holy Ghost conviction when it goes against the direct order of how God created the body to function.

Idol worship is something that must be broken off. There were certain gods that were worshipped by the ancestors where the worshippers engaged in sexual activity that was not in covenant with God. These idols were worshipped, and the sacrifices were then given to Jehovah or eaten by the people; all these are sins. A few idols that were an abomination to God were Ashtoreth, Chemosh, and Milcom (2 Kin. 23:13). In worship practices, children might have been passed through fire; homosexuality, fornication, and other sexual practices were rendered to reverence these gods. These forms of idol worship must be pulled down and destroyed so the generational curses will not continue to remain rooted in your bloodline. Now that you are saved and have the authority of the Holy Spirit, you can pull down strongholds and break generational curses off your life and the life of your descendants.

When it comes to curses and spiritual warfare, I suggest you be filled with the Holy Spirit before you engage in spiritual warfare. Once you receive salvation, and confess Christ, the Holy Spirit is the gift Jesus sends. The Spirit testified and is proof that He is risen from the dead and seated on the right hand of God (John 15:26). Pray asking to receive the Holy Spirit and it will be given to you. As I mentioned earlier, I was at home when I received the in-filling of the Holy Spirit. I have seen people filled for the first time in church. My good friend and I hold the "ReFresh Me" conference and people receive the in-filling of the Holy Ghost. The Holy Spirit gives utterance and knows how to pray when we do not. Romans 8:26 states, "Likewise the Spirit also helpeth our infirmities: for we know not what we should pray for as we ought: but the Spirit itself maketh intercession for us with groanings which cannot be uttered." There are deliverance ministries nationwide. My suggestion is that you do not open doors to engage the enemy if you're not prepared to fight.

Disclaimer submitted, now let's get the Vaseline and battle!

Prayer

Father, thank You for giving me my weapons of warfare. With the authority I have been given by the blood of Jesus Christ and the victory of His resurrection, I claim victory over every generational curse that my ancestors insurrected against the One Holy God Jehovah. I break every generational curse of fornication, bestiality, homosexuality, sodomy, sacrificing children in fire, sexual sacrificing of children, and any worship that was done in honor of idols. I say the jurisdiction is over and I take the authority of the demon that is a strong hold of my generation going back twenty-three hundred generations. Every idol that was planted in the lands and every abomination that was done under every tree, in every tent and high place, I pull it down in the name of Jesus Christ. Where there has been any shedding of blood in order to make covenant with the devil, I break the contract and call it void in the name of Jesus Christ. As for me and my house, we will serve the Lord. In Jesus' name. Amen!

EXPERIENCE 1: TEMPTED

Once you're delivered it will seem as if everything and the kitchen sink is being thrown at you. That's a testament! If you've truly repented and turned from sin and are making your best effort to steer clear of what had you bound, then the bullseye is on you. The enemy wants you to give up! He doesn't want yet another reminder that his time to reign in the earth is limited before he and his minions are cast into hell FOREVER.

Jesus says in Revelation 3:9-10:

> Behold, I will make them of the synagogue of Satan, which say they are Jews, and are not, but do lie; behold, I will make them to come and worship before thy feet, and to know that I have loved thee. Because thou hast kept the word of my patience, I also will keep thee from the hour of temptation, which shall come upon all the world, to try them that dwell upon the earth.

There are so many promises for those who try to operate in holiness. It's a lifestyle. When you desire to do what's right and honorable before God, people will look at you funny. God's way tends to conflict with the world norms and what is deemed acceptable. God's standards are high.

It's like you have luxury items you're housing but someone brings in dirty animals and muddy boots and tramples all over your upscale décor. You're going to be ticked off and feel like you're disrespected. Same with God! He has the top of the line; He has the best of the best but the world will try to downgrade what He has to make it seem like you're not going to get to enjoy it on earth, or try to make you believe there's no heaven or hell. The devil is a liar trying to swindle you out of your promises!

"Blessed is the man that endureth temptation: for when he is tried, he shall receive the crown of life, which the Lord hath promised to them that love him." (Jas. 1:12) "Endureth temptation" means "stands against it and gets past it". Jesus gives you the tool of success. "Endureth" and don't fall into the trap. Take His ways of escape and resist those urges and that unction that will try to entice you to fall back into your old sinful ways. Jesus has a crown with your name on it. Just resist until the end of your days.

Jesus was tempted of the devil and offered up a way to combat the devil. He showed us how to use the Word of God to do just that. You can simply say "Jesus!" if those urges come up, that person calls, or you're traveling near that place of vulnerability. Hebrews 2:18 says, "For in that he himself hath suffered being tempted, he is able to succor them that are tempted." "Succor" sounds like me with my country twang trying to say secure. According to *Webster's New World Dictionary*, the word *succor* means "to assist in times of hardship and distress". I haven't seen once in the Word where Jesus has left someone who is crying out or doesn't know how to help themselves. He is a present help, always!

There was a time when Jesus was praying and the disciples kept falling asleep. Sleeping on your post and not praying and seeking God leaves you vulnerable, and the enemy can do a sneak attack. Jesus had this to say, "Watch and pray, that ye enter not into temptation: the spirit indeed is willing, but the flesh is weak." (Matt. 26:41)

Prayer

Father, all praise unto You for giving us the weapons to surpass the enemy in the hour of temptation. Sharpen my discernment so that I can see the enemy and his devices far off. Root me in Your Word so that I can be like a tree planted by rivers of water. Sustain me in my hours of weakness. Uphold me by Your Holy Spirit. Teach me how to pray effectively. Embed Your Word in my mind, heart, and soul. Help me to resist the devil so that he may flee from me and to continue to resist all the days of my life. In Jesus' name. Amen!

EXPERIENCE 2: INSOMNIA

In therapy you can be taught your triggers. Yes, a great therapist can help you deal and heal! You know – those things that make you pop, burst into tears, and act mean and vicious to loved ones. It's the same with sin; the need to indulge in certain sins involves triggers, or moments, where the need to do these things is heightened. It can be a feeling that comes over you and the next thing you know, you're picking up the phone, getting to yourself, or getting in your car on the hunt to fulfill that desire that is now burning within you.

We are going to be really transparent when we say "burning", because there have been moments where my stomach hurt and I felt as if my groin would jump out of its place if I didn't satisfy the lusts of my flesh. DO YOU HEAR ME? Well, do you read me?

You can't hide anything within your heart, so remain bare-naked with truth in front of God. There is not a thing the devil can hold over your head to make you ashamed. God gives grace for your *weakness*, not the wickedness inside of you. There are people in the Bible who are considered "tares." Read the entire thirteenth chapter of Matthew to get a full understanding of a tare. A tare is someone that comes up with you, looks just like a person, but is from the other one and is evil just as their father, the devil.

While on the road to transfiguration, there will be people who will no longer walk with you, talk with you, or associate with you. That's okay! When there is a change for the good, or bad, people fall away. Just be prepared for that and go through the grieving process of those relationships, but don't allow grief to stay there. When rooted, it becomes a torment.

This leads us to address insomnia: those nights when sleep doesn't come and you find your fingers in your night clothes or that ex or prostitute in your bed or wherever. Yes, Insomnia — that good posse member to Lust — can have you doing odd things because you can't sleep. "An orgasm is the best nighttime medicine," Lust says, and the next thing you know you have toys coming out of the woodwork to help you rest easy.

When Lust or any member of its crew tries to rear its head, you must be quick to shut it down. That's the only way you will stay delivered and without shame. Am I saying you will not mess up? NO! What I am saying is you must be willing to pick up your weapons and fight to keep your house swept clean.

Proverbs 3:24 reads, "When thou liest down, thou shalt not be afraid: yea, thou shalt lie down, and thy sleep shall be sweet." Reading the text from verse 21 to 26 can also help after a home invasion or a series of nightmares. I love a two-for!

There are hours in the night when we are more sensitive and dream the most. We must protect ourselves with prayer before we sleep, and here's a suggestion: turn the television off. It's hard for those who need white noise to relax, but if it's not a Bible app talking scripture, then you're not completely turning your mind off, and you're also allowing your ear gates to be open and things entering your subconscious without your knowledge. Think about that!

Another scripture says, "When I remember thee upon my bed, and meditate on thee in the night watches. Because thou hast been my help, therefore in the shadow of thy wings will I rejoice. My soul followeth hard after thee: thy right hand upholdeth me." (Psa. 63:6-8) Acknowledging that your help comes from God is a way to have Him eager to come to your defense in the weakest moments. We all have them, but that is when we must allow Jesus to intercede on our behalf and allow God to be our strength.

It must be clear: there will be tests and trials we will face when trying to maintain freedom from certain sins. You may slip and fall, but there is a foundation that you're to come back to. There are tools we must use to maintain a consistent walk with Christ. When I turned from God, it was a choice. If I felt like I wanted to rush my process and do things my way, I would do an about-face. I sure did have to face the consequences of my actions, but there was more love when I returned to who I belonged to in the first place. God's love is infinite. Your problem in your flesh is not insignificant to the point that you can't ask God for help. He is NEVER too busy to answer every cry you have.

When insomnia has taped your eyelids to your brows, just reflect on the scriptures. Say them aloud to be encouraged. A prayer partner isn't always available, but Jesus always has an ear out and open, ready to help. Calling on the Father is your way of escape. Just like falling into the choice of sin is your right. We have a choice to do right or to do wrong. It's the part of us that wants to do wrong that is the loudest. Silence that part of your members with scripture. One in particular reads:

> I cried with my whole heart; hear me, O Lord: I will keep thy statutes. I cried unto thee; save me, and I shall keep thy testimonies. I prevented the dawning of the morning, and cried: I hoped in thy word. Mine eyes prevent the night watches, that I might meditate in thy word. Hear my voice according unto thy lovingkindness: O Lord, quicken me according to thy judgment. (Psa. 119:145-149)

Resisting and not falling into the sleeping pill of lust will not have you in regret in the morning. Resisting will not have you at the clinic, in a fight with someone else's spouse, or in depression because you feel you failed. Lean on God and use His Word as a weapon. Read the Word of God regularly and be not easily discouraged because of what unbelievers might tell you. Make your calling sure and know He is the God of your salvation.

Prayer

Father in heaven, we pray for rest and perfect peace as we slumber and sleep. We come against the noise of worry, doubt, unbelief, anxiety, depression, and night terrors in the name of Jesus. As we lay our heads to rest, God, help our minds to be fixed on You. Peace, be still in the name of Jesus. We shut the mouth of every demonic force that will try to infiltrate the atmosphere above our heads and below our beds in the name of Jesus. Every root, witchcraft, or warlock spirit or enchantment that has been set in the atmosphere around us, we return to the sender in the name of Jesus. Every night terror or nightmare of things of the past, we bind in the name of Jesus. Matthew 18:18 says whatsoever we bind on earth shall be bound in heaven. We loose a spirit of peace from our Jehovah Shalom. We decree fresh oil on our heads while we slumber and sleep in the name of Jesus. Amen!

EXPERIENCE 3: REJECTION

Who loves a good dose of rejection? No one! This is a perfect member to add to Lust's posse to keep you feeling down, cast aside, and alone, as if no one wants you around. Rejection has a posse of its own, but it fits great with Lust because being dumped, treated badly, overlooked, and removed from ties makes us vulnerable.

We must remember that Jesus was rejected in the worst way. Scripture reads, "And the Word was made flesh, and dwelt among us, (and we beheld his glory, the glory as of the only begotten of the Father,) full of grace and truth." (John 1:14) He was lied on, abandoned by his followers, whipped and beaten, crucified, and left for dead. If you have experienced something similar, then rely on Jesus! He was just who He said He was. The Savior of all who has all power! If you endure in Him then He will never forsake you or leave you lonely in your time of need.

Rejection can come by a choice. We can get clear direction and indication of how a situation will play out because history has proven this to be so. For example, you have a type you like to date. This type has brought about the same results. You're not receiving ANY of your desires out of these relationships, yet you end up with the same type of person time after time. There's now a cycle of rejection and hurt on top of hurt to the point where this type of person can spot you a mile away. Certain spirits attract each other because they have a posse they travel with. That's why the people you date are the same person, just with a different face.

These things that give you temporary fulfillment hold nothing but grief; they stifle your growth. "And he said unto them, Full well ye reject the commandment of God, that ye may keep your own tradition." (Mark 7:9) Here, Jesus is speaking to the Pharisees and Scribes about their being hypocrites with hearts far from God. In our rejection and hurt we tend to turn from God and do things our own way. This allows us to get in God's way when it comes to our deliverance and making us free from the past hurts and cycles that cause this behavior.

The weapon against rejection is confidence. Having confidence will block you from several forces and bad choices. When you're confident you don't accept any foolishness a user will put in your ear. "Trust ye not in a friend, put ye not confidence in a guide: keep the doors of thy mouth from her that lieth in thy bosom." (Mic. 7:5) Ladies, that goes for a man too. When you're used to being rejected, you lean on that glimmer of hope that this person will be "the one", only to find that when you confide in that person, they turn all you shared against you.

It's time to build self-worth! There must be deliverance and a shift in your way of thinking. I got into one of my most recent relationships to prove that I wasn't the person my ex-husband thought I was. Why are you trying to prove something to a person with whom you're no longer occupying physical space? We do that! Proving it to that other person is a front. We are really trying to prove to ourselves that we are not a bad person and we can love anyone. The reality is, our need for love is just desperation and we have drowned out the voice of God, who gives clear instructions on how to find a mate. One hundred percent of the work starts within!

Seeking a spouse comes with pre-work, pre-prep, and a God-head relationship first. In order to have a union ordained by the Father, you must have a personal relationship with Him. That's the pre-work. Makes sense to get to know the One who created the one He has for you, doesn't it?

The pre-prep is when you get your house in order. Paying off old debt. Doing away with toxic relationships that contradict what you wish to have in life. For example, I had a friend that said she wanted to be married and have a stable family for her and her child. Then she went and got her a 'friends with benefits' relationship. They didn't go on dates; she wasn't introduced to the family as 'the future Mrs' but was kept a secret. I had asked her, "If you want a union that you make a promise before your loved ones and God to be with this one person, and you go through the public process of changing your name and updating insurance and all your info, why are you doing the opposite of what you want?" Allow God to show you the areas of your life that need that pre-prep for you to be ready for such an important step as marriage.

Let's continue with the confidence-booster scriptures, shall we? "It is better to trust in the Lord than to put confidence in man." (Psa. 118:8) "Man" is used here in the sense that covers all humankind. A follow-up reads, "It is better to trust in the Lord than to put confidence in princes." (Psa. 118:9) Don't believe in that person who will remove all your debt and feel like you will not owe them your soul in the end. There is truly a Boaz in male and female form out there; however, you must work to meet them and accept wise counsel to get them, trust and keep God first in order to keep them.

We can move to the book of Proverbs, which states, "Confidence in an unfaithful man in time of trouble is like a broken tooth, and a foot out of joint." (Prov. 25:19) I've had to have two root canals, so I'm very familiar with a toothache, but to have a foot out of joint carrying my body weight in addition to that pain is unbearable. Reject rejection and lean on the Lord's everlasting arm!

"For the Lord shall be thy confidence, and shall keep thy foot from being taken." (Prov. 3:26) We can continue in Proverbs, reading, "In the fear of the Lord is strong confidence: and his children shall have a place of refuge." (Prov. 14:26) What a great comfort in knowing that God has everything we need and He will not refuse us? Combat rejection by building a wall of refuge around yourself that's protected by the mighty hand of God.

That's not to say cast it out of your mind, but learn what triggers you. Learn the emotions and feelings that come up that will have you in that place of rejection. Once you see the pattern you can know what strategy to use to fight. The enemy doesn't come with a different trick, but the tricks are disguised in different ways based on our unique emotions. If you're feeling ultimate joy, the devil will bring up memories or triggers of times you were unhappy. If you're sad already, the enemy will use triggers that compound that feeling to make it overwhelming for you. Knowing the devices and getting self-control will have the devil on his back every time.

Prayer

Father, we come asking for a boldness to stand against the adversary like we never have before. Unlike before, we are confident in You. Unlike before, we know we have all power since Christ is risen. We have faith and believe we can press toward the mark of our calling in Christ Jesus. We are confident that in Your house is many mansions and Your Son Christ has gone ahead to make a place for us. We know that we know that we know we can do greater works because Christ is alive and Your Holy Spirit dwells within us. We pray that You continue the work in our deliverance and open our minds to understand the freedom and liberty we have in Christ. Teach us how to use the weapons we have in our artillery and make us bold in Your Word. In Jesus' name. Amen!

EXPERIENCE 4: REGRET

When we think of getting some R&R, we think of rest and relaxation, right? We discussed Rejection, but a posse member named Regret is there to whisper the should've, could've, would've. I should've asked a friend to come out with me, walk home with me, or meet me, then I wouldn't have been raped. I could've used protection, now I have HIV. If I would've listened when God told me to go right, things wouldn't be so wrong.

Regret is a spirit. Regret regrets following the devil and believing he could be a supreme being above the Great Almighty. Regret wishes it made a different decision when the opportunity was presented. Unlike that spirit, you are a living soul! I know because you're reading this book and working through the pages with your own writing with a hunger and thirst to get back to God. There is still opportunity because you have breath. Don't take it for granted! Start now. Start today. Don't wait on tomorrow; the only guarantee in this life is death. You don't know when it will come for you, so be ready!

We serve a God who isn't out of reach. When God looks on your regret or your contrite spirit, He is near. "The Lord is nigh unto them that are of a broken heart; and saveth such as be of a contrite spirit." (Psa. 34:18) When you need to beg for forgiveness, Psalm 51 is the one you can read aloud and plug all your shortcomings into and get to God's ear and pierce His heart. Your heart, however, must be prepared for the turning – the change that is to occur in you when you repent. Specifically, it says, "The sacrifices of God are a broken spirit: a broken and contrite heart, O God, thou wilt not despise." (Psa. 51:17)

Being nice to people will not get you into heaven; confessing Jesus is the ONLY way to get there. If you have unforgiveness in your heart toward others and yourself, then how can you see God? It's a daily task to live right and confess things that God is trying to work out of you. His desire is to have ALL His children return to Him. He gave us a choice. We must choose Him. He has given us everything we need to make it, but we allow influences outside of our relationship with God to complicate the union. It's easier to be in a marriage when you're not accepting everyone's opinion about you and your partner. Not everyone hears God the same. Not everyone has the same convictions. Not everyone has the same level of discernment. You can't follow a person on their path aimlessly because it's not yours. It's personal!

This is what God said through the Prophet Isaiah:

> For thus saith the high and lofty One that inhabiteth eternity, whose name is Holy; I dwell in the high and holy place, with him also that is of a contrite and humble spirit, to revive the spirit of the humble, and to revive the heart of the contrite ones. (Isa. 57:15)

You read it right. God dwells with your regret-filled, sorrowful, guilty, and full-of-repentance self. That's not the first time in the Word that God says He makes His dwelling with man. That's your homework: find the other place where God said He would dwell with you, and He said He will bring Jesus along too. Where They are there is action, so you know the Holy Ghost is rolling also.

Regret adds sorrow. You hate that you're breathing. You hate that you're single. You hate who you married. Know that "The blessing of the Lord, it maketh rich, and he addeth no sorrow with it." (Prov. 10:22) We are not talking about monetary riches. Being rich in faith, longsuffering, confidence, peace, hope, and all the other fruit of the spirit – that's what makes you really rich. When there is an abundance in God's spirit, there is no regret; there is no room for sorrow. He will turn your mourning into dancing.

We make a trail of destruction when we do things our way. Most of the time we make a mess that we ourselves can't clean up. The big God we serve gives a grace mop that allows us to get it right with

Him. Doing this will in turn get it right with those you wronged. It's up to the person you wronged to get deliverance from the sting of the hurt, but it's your responsibility to get forgiveness and its fullness for yourself. **Your happiness is your responsibility.** Your victory over Lust and its posse is your responsibility. No one can get you through this life but Jesus, but it's your responsibility to let Him in when He knocks. It's your responsibility not to push Him out of your house once you make up your mind that you want to go backwards and do things your own way. The Word says, "So shalt thou put away the guilt of innocent blood from among you, when thou shalt do that which is right in the sight of the Lord." (Deut. 21:9)

Why are we back on forgiveness and the wrong we cause others? Regret will attach to situations and you will try in your own strength to right the wrong you caused. You can live in regret for how you treated a good person for years and miss the people God is putting in your path now for fear of getting close or allowing people in because it's the law that you reap what you sow. At least, that's how you're looking at it. You must pray, "Deliver me from all my transgressions: make me not the reproach of the foolish." (Psa. 39:8) Your reproach or regret will have you in shame. It can have you heavy and in a depressed state that you can't shake. "Reproach hath broken my heart; and I am full of heaviness: and I looked for some to take pity, but there was none; and for comforters, but I found none." (Psa. 69:20) Friends will be few and far between once you allow regret to take root. No one wants to go to a pity party. That is not a celebration!

Regret will have you in isolation and where there is isolation comes Suicide. Every spirit has a posse. It's like a tree that has roots. Once you pull up the root of that tree, it cannot grow and have branches and bear fruit. Lust is the root we are getting deliverance from in this book. The posse that we are mentioning in the experience portion are the branches. If Lust is the root, Regret the branch, and Isolation the leaves, that makes Suicide the fruit. That's why certain things we accept are so destructive. It's a little sin today but give it time to take root. You will see how it manifests. My prayer for this work is that you will be able to spot the enemy and his devices. You will be effective in your prayers to the point where these spirits will not take root and cause destruction or death. It's not death by suicide that I'm speaking of, but death of the kind of spiritual life that leads to eternity with the Holy Trinity. Eternity is a long time. If you think watching the clock on Friday waiting on time to go home takes forever, then don't chance your everlasting life!

Regret will have you in condemnation or disapproval of self. Everything you do, even when it's a great thing… you will find fault in it. There will be something wrong with the deed, the process, or the results. Regret will have you looking down on your whole life. It will have you displaying a doom and gloom mentality because you are reliving past decisions and their outcome. We know this is a spirit because it was by the Spirit of God that Peter could confess Christ was who He said He was before the resurrection (Matt 16:16-17).

> For there are certain men [(spirits)] crept in unawares, who were before of old ordained to this condemnation, ungodly men, turning the grace of our God into lasciviousness, and denying the only Lord God, and our Lord Jesus Christ. (Jude v. 4)

We are taught in 1 John 2:22 that if one denies Christ, they also deny God. This is the antichrist and completely goes against the fruit of the spirit that a person displays once a relationship with Christ is cultivated. The spirit of Satan is lawless and will have you denying the true and living God. Don't allow regret to fix your lips to turn God's blessing into ashes. Do not allow your lips to pervert what God has blessed. Walk into your deliverance and stand right there!

We may need deliverance from things we did in our youth that have led us astray from the presence of God. Regretting that you committed the offense and not trying to resolve it with the Father can have you complacent, stagnant, and lacking growth. A defeated spirit can't get victory. Accept what you have done, repent, and work hard to turn from it. If God brings a situation to your memory that is in need of repentance, do it quickly. Confess it immediately! Do not risk a life of peace and everlasting life of pure joy with Jehovah because you're too ashamed to admit your faults.

> Rejoice, O young men, in thy youth, and let thy heart cheer thee in the days of thy youth, and walk in the ways of thine heart, and in the sight of thine eyes: but know thou, that for all these things God will bring thee into judgment. Therefore

> remove sorrow from thy heart, and put away evil from thy flesh: for childhood and youth are vanity. (Eccl. 11:9-10)

"Vanity", as used here, means it's not eternal; it will pass away. Scripture tells you to remove sorrow from your heart. If it's in the Word, then it is possible, and it is in your power to do so. Jesus returned to the Father so that we can have a shot at everlasting life. He also left us with the power to be conquerors in His name with the indwelling of the Holy Spirit.

I had to confess my regret for getting married and the fact that I had a baby with a husband I really didn't know. I regret how it ended and thought constantly about how my life would've been different if I had married the right person. I was unaware that regretting carrying that person's seed was cursing my seed directly. Your thoughts are the happening before the action takes place. If you think evil, sooner or later evil will be done by you. "For as he thinketh in his heart, so is he: Eat and drink, saith he to thee; but his heart is not with thee." (Prov. 23:7)

If I allowed that regret to fester; if I had chosen to not get delivered and confess that thing when the Holy Spirit brought it to my attention, there is no telling what kind of mother I would be today. Mothers and fathers don't become hateful evil people over night. There is something that happened to them in the past that took root and is manifesting itself through them. Do your work so you can be better not just for those around you or who are attached to you, but do it for your own peace.

Prayer

Lord, in the name of Jesus, I ask You to remove all sorrow of heart. I ask You to remove the sting of the hurt of every situation that made me forfeit my walk with Christ. Forgive me, God, for allowing situations and people to repeat themselves when we were full or unaware. God, remove the pride of life; remove the need to feel in control. God, You are the head of my life. Take Your rightful place in my heart. Remove regret. I cast it into the pits of hell never to rise again. Every bad decision, past decisions regarding harming myself and others, I repent in the name of Jesus. Lift the burden of sorrow off my heart, remove the memory from my mind in the name of Jesus. Have Your way, God. Fill me up, God, and occupy the space where those unclean spirits dwelt. In Jesus' name.
Amen!

EXPERIENCE 5: BITTERNESS

Bitterness can have you hating the world, your parents, your kids, and even yourself. You can be with who you want, be where you want to be in life, but still be in a place of bitterness. Your life can be planned out then if it didn't go according to your plans, and you're mad about it. Let's look at the definition, shall we?

Webster's New World Dictionary defines *bitterness* as "the anger and disappointment at being treated unfairly; resentment." I doubt there is a person on earth who hasn't been treated unfairly. It's the person who is close who can cause wounds that open the ground for that seed to be planted, take root, and sprout. Next thing you know, you are hell to deal with and just angry all the time, and the foul things that come out of your mouth make it seem like you were raised in the wild and have no clue who God is.

You must get to the root — the entry point — in order to pluck it out of your soul.

> Follow peace with all men, and holiness, without which no man shall see the Lord: Looking diligently lest any man fail of the grace of God; lest any root of bitterness springing up trouble you, and thereby many be defiled; Lest there be any fornicator, or profane person, as Esau, who for one morsel of meat sold his birthright. (Heb. 12:14-16)

The scripture is just how it happens… when it says "bitterness springing up"! As if you didn't know it was there before.

I mentioned in the last chapter how I had that regret because my marriage ended in divorce and I was a single parent. I didn't wait in celibacy ten years before marriage just to end up alone again, and on top of that raise a child by myself. That was not my plan! I didn't know the posse was dwelling within until the Holy Spirit had me confess about being angry, full of regret, and bitter toward my ex-husband and my daughter. I had no idea this was within! It sprung up as the scripture said.

The treatment in my marriage was horrible and became violent. I was thinking God was going to change him because I chose him. I didn't wait on the green light from God to get married; I just did it because I got tired of waiting. That decision produced a chain of events that made me bitter. Years had gone by, but I was still picking men with the same characteristics – the same spirit! I was with these men to prove I wasn't who my ex-husband said I was. I had to prove I could love again and be open to love. Why did I feel I had to prove it?

That question took me to my childhood. It took me to that grandparent who made it known I was not her favorite and that I was only good enough to attract a man with a good job to take care of me because she felt I wasn't that smart. It damaged my self-esteem. My confidence was shot! It wasn't until I was in college that my literature professor told me I should take up writing. It wasn't even on my radar. I wrote poetry for years, drew pictures, and wrote songs but I didn't share them with the world. I only shared the recreation of a story in that particular class because it was a heavily weighted grade. We can be in our purpose and practicing our purpose but with lack of confidence we don't see what the Lord is doing.

I turned a dreadful story into a comedy for that project. The professor read it aloud. She didn't tell us whose she was reading, but when she started reading the part we were supposed to change, I sank in my seat. This woman and the class were in tears laughing by the end. She said it was the creativity in the twist and the details that made me a good writer and storyteller. She told me to reconsider a writing career if it wasn't my choice. Here I am four books later if you include this one.

I have a question: what do you feel like you must prove? It. The thing that would allow you to be equal or worth it in the eyes of the person who isn't thinking about what you do day to day. Why are you stuck? Why are you full of resentment? Why are you holding the weight of bitterness that has left you alone emotionally and cut off?

Life is full of obstacles. You will be disappointed, especially in people. Married or not, people have their own agenda and life, so you must make it a point to be happy. Happiness is a choice and staying bitter, angry, and disappointed is a choice. What do you do about all these emotions? "Let all bitterness, and wrath, and anger, and clamour, and evil speaking, be put away from you, will all malice: And be ye kind one to another, tenderhearted, forgiving one another, even as God for Christ's sake hath forgiven you." (Eph. 4:31-32) Forgiveness! A common theme throughout this work and in life.

Do not forget to forgive yourself. When I confessed the regret and bitterness I was holding against my ex and my child and asked for forgiveness unto the Father, I felt a weight lifted off me. There were snot and tears and total release. It was very necessary! I had to let go of what that family member thought of me because it affected my marriage. Once I was divorced and had to pray my way out of a dark depression while caring for a child with no money, job, or other resources, back living with my parents when I had been on my own since age 19, it felt like failure. It wasn't what people expected of Ilaya. Somewhere in my deliverance the question came up: *whose expectations are you carrying?* When I realized they were not my own, I had to drop the chains. I had to dig in my soul to see what it was that bound me.

Since then, I have been living off what *God* expects of me. That is obedience. Have I gotten it right every step of the way? Heck no! I have goals I wish to accomplish in this life, not expectations. After that period, I felt free. Prayer works. Getting in the Word works. Allowing the Holy Spirit to show you the areas that are a hindrance and letting them go WORKS! It's great to serve a God who is alive and a present help.

"Repent therefore of this thy wickedness, and pray God, if perhaps the thought of thine heart may be forgiven thee. For I perceive that thou art in the gall of bitterness, and in the bond of iniquity." (Acts 8: 22-23) The scripture says you may be bound by the gall of bitterness. It's hard for God to get work out of you when there are spirits warring against the work He wishes to do *in* you. Unforgiveness hinders the works of God, but more importantly, it hinders your access to the kingdom of God. If you wish to get to the mansion Jesus went to prepare for you, then you must allow Him to have a complete work within you.

Whatever your age, think of yourself as a car. Just go with me for a moment, okay? You're a car. Me? I'm a 35-year-old car. A person (God) hands you a credit card that doesn't have a limit. He then says "Car, go to My Mechanic and allow Him to do the work on you." There is no need to worry about operating hours because the Shop is open 24 hours a day and never closes. You're not restricted by cost and your budget because your Source has no limits. You have full knowledge of the resource you have, but you decide to try to fix things yourself. You don't make time to go get the work done and you're broken down and busted on the side of the road and the person who has to tow you to that Shop is looking at you crazy because they see your unlimited access to the best Shop in the world on the dashboard.

That is how crazy you look when you don't seek the Lord for help! Once you're saved, you have access to the Holy Spirit. Once filled, you receive power! Why not go for the gusto and get all that belongs to you! You know it's yours because Christ said it would be. Don't allow the warfare of the enemy to talk you out of your deliverance even now!

Allow the scriptures to take root in you. When we do the prayer, take that time and allow the prayer that you have spoken aloud to penetrate the atmosphere and give the Holy Spirit time to work in you so that He can work that unclean thing out of you. The goal is to be released and free! He whom the Son sets free is free indeed (John 8:36).

There are times when you must wear a mask in order to keep some things between yourself and God. I'm not saying you're trying to deceive the world and present yourself as something or someone you're not; what I'm saying is that you can't try to get your deliverance in a public setting with everyone looking on. You have priorities and this mask must be on when you're in your role as a worker, a parent, or a spouse, but this work — your deliverance — takes your time and dedication because it's going to take just that to keep it. The mask is you having to hold life together in order to function in this world despite all the things you and God are working out in secret. This workbook is so that you can bare it all and be your real self – flaws and all! You must read your Word consistently; pray consistently. There will be stumbling and skinned knees, but God will forgive you and His grace is sufficient for you.

Prayer

Father, in the name of Jesus, I denounce the power of the words that were spoken over me, the treatment that was unfair, the memory that activates my rage. I pull them down and cast them into the pits of hell. Pull out every root of bitterness and all demons that come with it. Every scar that it leaves, seal it with Your blood, Jesus! I pray that the people whom I allowed into my soul – that door will be closed and sealed with the blood of Jesus. I repent of harboring unforgiveness and strife. I repent of the actions that I did while bitterness was full-blown. I release every fiery dart of bitterness, malice, anger, and disappointment from my life, from my soul, and from by bloodline. Heal every bruise and close the breach between You and me, Jesus. In Jesus' name I pray. Amen!

EXPERIENCE 6: LOW SELF-ESTEEM

- "I will praise thee; for I am fearfully and wonderfully made: marvelous are thy works; and that my soul knoweth right well." (Psa. 139:14)
- "Before I formed thee in the belly I knew thee; and before thou camest forth out of the womb I sanctified thee, and I ordained thee a prophet unto the nations." (Jer. 1:5)
- "One thing have I desired of the Lord, that will I seek after; that I may dwell in the house of the Lord all the days of my life, to behold the beauty of the Lord, and to enquire in his temple." (Psa. 27:4)
- "It is better to trust in the Lord than to put confidence in man." (Psa. 118:8)
- "For the Lord shall be thy confidence, and shall keep thy foot from being taken." (Prov. 3:26)
- "And this is the confidence that we have in him that, if we ask any thing according to his will, he heareth us: And if we know that he hear us, whatsoever we ask, we know that we have in petitions that we desired of him." (1 John 5:14)

Dumping scripture is key in this experience. When you struggle to see your beauty, worth, and life in your reflection, you need to see how God sees you. Low self-esteem is a killer of your spirit. It can deceive you into thinking you're not worth the air you breathe, and that you don't have talents that are worth talking about.

I went to Savannah College of Art and Design for a semester. They were big on students presenting their work in a presentation. The school had the understanding that if you were going into business or getting a job you needed to be able to articulate on your own behalf. I would downgrade every piece of art, every project, and every work I created that semester. There was a guy in the class, another student, who would get annoyed with my presentations. He would sigh heavily and roll his eyes. One day after class he stopped me. He informed me that I had great ideas and an amazing artistic eye, but I didn't believe in myself. It came across in my presentation. He told me it would be better if I didn't say anything, because when I spoke it killed the beauty of my work. He wasn't being mean; students were told to give a critique. I had already been critiqued and compared all my life, so accepting criticism wasn't anything unfamiliar. This was the first time I realized my low self-esteem had a major effect on my gifts, and it was to the point that I could no longer hide it with comedy.

You need to know you're enough. You need to be reminded of your access. Get these scriptures in your spirit! The devil will try to tell you that God has no use for you and God allowed everything to happen to you. Your warfare aligns with your destiny. The bigger the demons you have been fighting all your life, the greater the work God has for you. Do you think God would've offered Job to be tested if He didn't know what He put in him to begin with?

Some of you have dealt with abuse sexually, physically, and emotionally. These things will work together for your good. You're an asset to the kingdom! What we must understand is that everyone has a choice to do good or to do evil. Their choice to do evil could've killed you but it didn't. I know that because you have this book in your hand and you want your deliverance. Your deliverance is not for you alone! That Shame, which is a spirit posse, is cast down today. You're not God's reject but His prized possession. He was with you in the tribulation; He has plans for you and those plans are perfect. In Jesus' name, I pray that the scales be removed from your eyes right now that you may see the plans the Father has for you when you see your reflection in the mirror. Amen!

The enemy has allowed people to think that once you receive salvation your life will be easy. That's why as soon as something gets rough, you feel like you can put Christ away. You've been deceived.

Jesus was tempted and died a horrible death. He was God and was with God and nothing was made that didn't include Him (John 1:1). We are not exempt; however, God always has a plan so what did He do to show He cared? "But God commendeth his love toward us, in that, while we were yet sinners, Christ died for us." (Rom. 5:8) God wants nothing more than for His children to come back to Him once this life is over. He wants nothing more than for us to see the God in us even though we bear the bumps and bruises of life. We will have scars, but those scars were not meant to kill us. Just as Jesus has scars from the nails, thorns, and the piercing in His side, but still lives, we will live because of His sacrifice.

There will be times when you will not be feeling it. All the emotions that come up – acknowledge them; allow them to come out; allow them to work through you and pass. Sometimes we hold on to things unaware because we think we're not supposed to have certain feelings and we rebuke the devil, but we rebuke our natural emotions that need to process through our hearts and minds so that we can be free. Emotions that are unaddressed become open doors that invite spirits to come on in. Unforgiveness is a major open door! We forget to forgive ourselves. Things happen to you, so that makes you a major part of the puzzle. We forgive other people and work through that process, but we don't address the feelings we harbor toward ourselves.

Once you build your confidence arsenal with the Word of God your overview in life will change because your self-reflection will change. You won't accept things people try to bring to you. You won't care who they are! It's not that you will be arrogant, but you will be confident in your capabilities and secure in your position with God. In this book alone, we said the sinner's prayer, took a praise break to receive the Holy Spirit, and now we are trying to maintain our deliverance. Accepting Christ is an instant confidence-booster because allowing Him to take the reins of your life brings assurance.

If you were saved before and backslidden, it's okay to get a refill. I had to get re-baptized. I was purged and I was filled with the Holy Spirit. It's a work in progress, my friend! Don't beat yourself up over your mistakes along the way. We are working toward perfection; we aren't perfect yet!

We must combat every negative thought and word that has been spoken over us throughout our life. Through His words to the prophet Jeremiah, this is what the Lord says of His thoughts of you:

> For I know the thoughts that I think toward you, saith the Lord, thoughts of peace, and not of evil, to give you an expected end. Then shall ye call upon me, and ye shall go and pray unto me, and I will hearken unto you. And ye shall seek me, and find me, when ye shall search for me with all your heart: (Jer. 29:11-13)

If God thinks highly enough of you to assure you that He will answer you when you call on His name with all your heart, then it stands, because God can't lie. Those friends, your parents, them kids, that spouse may lie — and lie repeatedly and not show up for you repeatedly — but God is forever present in your life. He just wants you to call on Him and keep calling on Him. Not just when you're in trouble, but because He is Abba Father and you just need to talk to Him.

Matthew 18:18 states, "Verily I say unto you, Whatsoever ye shall bind on earth shall be bound in heaven: and whatsoever ye shall loose on earth shall be loosed in heaven." You know it's true because it's written in red in the Word. That's Jesus talking! He is handing out authority throughout the pages and it's up to us to put that authority into action. You do that by using the Word of God.

I had to bind the words that were spoken over me by saying, "I bind the words *whore*, *stupid*, *uneducated*, being told I would never be anything, and I loose the mind of Christ in my mind. I loose a spirit of boldness. I loose a spirit of joy. In the name of Jesus." I repeated that thing until I believed it. There were other words that would come up as I did this continually. The more I did it, the freer I got! The lighter I felt. The more I spoke these words over myself, the more I believed I was a prized possession and worthy of love. I cut people off faster when I noticed they didn't hold me in the same esteem I held myself. You get bold in the Lord, y'all!

- "I can do all things through Christ which strengtheneth me." (Phil. 4:13)
- "There hath no temptation taken you but such as common to man: but God is faithful, who will not suffer you to be tempted above that ye are able; but will with the

temptation also make a way to escape, that ye may be able to bear it." (1 Cor. 10:13) He helps you get away! Just take the door.

- "Come unto me, all ye that labour and are heavy laden, and I will give you rest. Take my yoke upon you, and learn of me; for I am meek and lowly in heart: and ye shall find rest unto your souls. For my yoke is easy, and my burden is light." (Matt. 11:28-30) This was out of Jesus' mouth. Give it to Him and allow Him to handle what you can't.

In this process of purging there will be things that come your way to test you, to make you turn back from your deliverance. When the Israelites escaped Egypt, they wanted to go back because things seemed hard, and they were not getting way. They would've chosen bondage over freedom in the Lord. This will be presented to you as well, but remember the Word says, "Trust in the Lord with all thine heart; and lean not unto thine own understanding. In all thy ways acknowledge him, and he shall direct thy paths." (Prov. 3:5-6)

We are going into prayer with this promise in the front of our mind. God says to Isaiah, the mouthpiece of the Lord:

> Fear thou not; for I am with thee: be not dismayed; for I am thy God: I will strengthen thee; yea, I will help thee; yea, I will uphold thee with the right hand of my righteousness. Behold, all they that were incensed against thee shall be ashamed and confounded: they shall be as nothing; and they that strive with thee shall perish. (Isa. 41:10-11)

Prayer

Father, You have made me exactly how I should be. I am who I should be. Your ways are not my ways and Your thoughts are not my thoughts. They are higher than mine. Remove every negative thought I have for myself. Remove every word that was negatively spoken over my head that was intended to steal, kill, and destroy my confidence. I curse the works of the enemy and the generational curses that have manifested themselves in my life. The curse of self- and child sacrifice, I break it in Jesus' name. Elevate the way I think of myself so that it may align with the way You think of me. Open my eyes so that I may see myself the way You see me. Open my ears so that my mind can receive how highly You speak of me. For I am made in Your image and everything that You made that was made, You called it good. I thank You that I'm good. I thank You that You knew me before I was born, and You set a good plan for me. God, I seek You so that You can place in me the confidence I need to have my destiny fulfilled in the earth. In Jesus' name. Amen!

EXPERIENCE 7: SENSUALITY

This next one is a doozy. When it came up in my spirit, I had to ask God for clarity, and this is what I received. When I was a wild child, I had a way of projecting my sexuality unto a person of interest. Example, when I was in the club, I wouldn't have to make eye contact; I would project from the inside of myself to the person I was interested in. Yes, it sounds like witchcraft and it very well could be classified as such. It was like the projection of pheromones to the brother with the shoulders and then he approaches.

Sounds crazy, but those who have a handle and have fine-tuned their sensuality craft know exactly what I'm talking about. Let's get the definition, shall we? Oxfordlearnersdictionaries.com defines *sensuality* as "the fact of giving pleasure to your physical senses, especially sexual pleasure; the enjoyment or expression of physical pleasure." It's the condition of being pleasing or fulfilling to the senses.

The unfortunate thing about sensuality is that pastors, teachers, and prophets (among other offices/workers in ministry) who haven't seen the deliverance necessary to be effective in ministry succumb to this and end up sleeping with church members and damaging the souls of the flock.

The best example of sensuality in the Bible is the book of First Samuel. The priest Eli had sons who would receive gifts for the temple of God and then sleep with the givers. Just a slew of sex and defiling the temple, all outside of the will of God. "Now the sons of Eli were sons of Belial; they knew not the Lord." (1 Sam. 2: 12) I'm sure you noticed that their first problem was that they were working in the house of the Lord but they did not know the Lord. There are preachers who are ministers of God, but they do not know Him. They go through the motions of religion and tickle your emotions to stimulate you, but they do not offer anything the Lord has commanded because He is not talking to them. They are doing all out of flesh! That feeling you got when you were sitting in the congregation, no matter how big or small, was discernment that the Spirit of God gives. You knew you were in the wrong place. Heed the Spirit of God and don't worry about which person is offended. Your main task is to not offend your God.

Eli's sons were supposed to be taking the offering and giving it to the Lord, but they were raising the portion required and taking the difference for themselves. Of course, this angered the Lord, because people no longer wanted to give their offering unto God because of the opposition. This is what else they had going on:

> Now Eli was very old, and heard all that his sons did unto all Israel; and how they lay with the women that assembled at the door of the tabernacle of the congregation. And he said unto them, Why do ye such things? for I hear of your evil dealings by all this people. Nay, my sons; for it is no good report that I hear: ye make the Lord's people to transgress." (1 Sam. 2: 22-24)

Sensuality is a form of seduction – the very root of it! If you have operated in this as I have in the past, then you're in tune with what I'm saying, and this resonates with you. This spirit creates soul ties and deep ones too. It will have people attached to you with the inability to release you. When someone is attached to you in this way, it adds weight to your spirit man, and it will be hard for you to get free as well. In this case, not only will you need deliverance, but you will need freedom from those with whom you have tied yourself along the course of your life.

It's a must that you walk in the right spirit. When feelings come up, do not cast them out of your mind but wait in that moment. God will reveal what it is that came up. For example, I projected my sensuality on a person by accident. Yes, it was done by accident. This person was not an interest and I was saved, but in my backsliding.

[Side note: when you're backslidden it's like you've taken off the armor of God and opened yourself to the darkness of sin.] Back to it! It happened because God needed to reveal what was still dwelling within. You can be saved and Holy Spirit-filled and still having unclean spirits. That's why Romans 7 is so prevalent to believers.

The fact that God revealed that to me allowed me to get deliverance and to pray effectively concerning my freedom and so that I could loose that person and every other person who has been victim to my lustful ways.

> This I say then, Walk in the Spirit, and ye shall not fulfil the lust of the flesh. For the flesh lusteth against the Spirit, and the Spirit against the flesh: and these are contrary the one to the other: so that ye cannot do the things that ye would. But if ye be led of the Spirit, ye are not under the law. (Gal. 5:16-18)

Sensuality is used for personal gain! There are some who can seduce a person out of their entire check, house, and all they possess. The sad thing is they feel they are in need or have placed their faith in material things that perish instead of locating the Savior and allowing Him to be that provider. This is the whole reason for this book. You've recognized your error and want to change course to get on the street called "Straight" and to become one with the Father. God said prophetically to me, "You're dismantling the altars you've erected when you acknowledge your sin and that you're not walking with Him, and the attempt to turn from that error is like worship to Him, and He will meet you there and take over!"

The spirit of Jezebel is prevalent and will have a nation fall into sin. Jezebel was in a marriage but wasn't the submissive one in the relationship. She was the roaring lion that wore the pants and was the unofficial ruler of the kingdom. Murder, fornication, and idol worship were the things she did. She would kill whoever told her "No." These things were done without permission of the king. That's the same thing we do! We operate outside the will of God and go against His authority due to our own desires and lusts. We're going to pray to set things in their true order.

Prayer

Father, my deliverer, I confess I have operated in a Jezebel spirit. I arrest Jezebel and cast her out of me in the name of Jesus. I have operated in a spirit of sensuality and seduction. Deliver me from the error of my ways. Deliver me from worshipping idols and from my evil ways. I put them away! Purge me from the demonic forces that I allowed to enter in with my seduction. Break every unholy soul tie that I have attached to or that has been attached to me. Break the chains of bondage off my life, my seed, and my remnant in the earth. Make me new and make me whole in the mighty name of Jesus. Take my life, oh God, and place it on the path of righteousness. Give me the discernment regarding when to pray. Sharpen the prayer within me so that I recognize the spirits that will try to entice me. Help me to call them by name and cast them out in Jesus' name! Amen.

EXPERIENCE 8: SEXUAL IMMORALITY

For the commandment is a lamp; and the law is light; and reproofs of instruction are the way of life:
To keep thee from the evil woman, from the flattery of the tongue of a strange woman.
Lust not after her beauty in thine heart; neither let her take thee with her eyelids.
For by means of a whorish woman a man is brought to a piece of bread: and the adultress will hunt for the precious life.
Can a man take fire in his bosom, and his clothes not be burned?
Can one go upon hot coals, and his feet not be burned?
So he that goeth in to his neighbour's wife; whosoever toucheth her shall not be innocent.
Men do not despise a thief, if he steal to satisfy his soul when he is hungry;
But if he be found, he shall restore sevenfold; he shall give all the substance of his house.
But whoso committeth adultery with a woman lacketh understanding: he that doeth it destroyeth his own soul.
A wound and dishonour shall he get; and his reproach shall not be wiped away.
For jealousy is the rage of a man: therefore he will not spare in the day of vengeance.
He will not regard any ransom; neither will he rest content,

> though thou givest many gifts. (Prov. 6:23-35)

That is a mouthful and a lot to read out the gate, but we needed to see the scripture to get the bigger picture. Man, or woman, can have sexual immorality and/or sexual impurity. Adultery is a major offense to God. The married couple is in covenant with Him. There is a spirit of sexual immorality/impurity that will attack marriages in order to allow entry of other spirits to make people break covenant.

There are people who can't get a handle on the fact that they only sleep with people who are married. This is their actual preference. We're touching on a lot in this book and the wounds are the reasoning for this person, but the root is they have a spirit, or demon, that they need deliverance from. The previous spirit posse members we discussed would have someone thinking being in such a relationship would prevent them from experiencing pain and boost their confidence because they can take what someone else's spouse. Similarly, these relationships can be an open display of low self-esteem because they feel this is the only relationship they can have. Wounds and past hurt are the access point for the spirits to enter. They piggy-back on the pain in that moment and start talking to you in order for you to accept a lawless mindset that completely contradicts the Word of God.

> Mortify therefore your members which are upon the earth; fornication, uncleanness, inordinate affection, evil concupiscence, and covetousness, which is idolatry: For which things' sake the wrath of God cometh on the children of disobedience: In the which ye also walked some time, when ye lived in them. (Col. 3:5-7)

This is a form of idol worship because the root of operating in these actions is of an idol, Baal. Baal worship edified the deity of fertility. Whenever you see Baal mentioned in the Bible there is fornication and mass sexual immorality. Rightfully so, if this is the god of fertility. The error with this is that there is no order of the Lord when doing these sexual practices. They're having orgies and sleeping with whomever. This is outside the will of God if you're to keep yourself pure and holy for one wife or husband. Serving other gods that are not the One Living God will make you an open portal to receive unclean spirits.

God constructed the family unit so there would be no confusion and so that you could trace your lineage. Every person is to know what they are made to do in the earth. You receive your first idea of this based on who your family is. For example, there is a family in my hometown where there are three generations of doctors. If there was an outside child raised by outside influences, then that outside child may not operate in their inheritance if they didn't know their lineage.

I'm not bashing children out of wedlock. If you received offense by the above example, ask God to free you of that shame or guilt and press in the Word of God. I'm divorced as well and have a child. My daughter is aware of who her father is and her family on his side. That is the point! It's not that children outside of wedlock do not have lineage, but it's better to teach a child by showing them daily where they came from and planting in them purpose. Amen!

Baal worship is the root! We can operate in idol worship unaware. Our participation in certain things is not spiritually sound, and we are ignorant because we are not praying and reading the Word of God as we should. Now, we have STD's — sexually transmitted demons — and need deliverance because we've attached ourselves to unclean practices. Let's get free! God is a deliverer. Jesus is the Way! We have worked through the process and are checking the boxes as we go through the work to make sure these things are done in order.

Accepting Christ is one; being filled with the Holy Spirit is His gift to you and number two; and three is building a relationship through the Word of God in order to get close to the Father to maintain your deliverance — that's the slide to home plate. Your relationship is paramount! You can come to a job every day and not know your CEO. You come to work and receive perfect attendance awards and all these accolades but never know who signed your check. That's how people's relationship with God is. They are operating out of religion but don't know who breathed life into them, and they are unaware their name is slowly fading out of the Book of Life.

"But fornication, and all uncleanness, or covetousness, let it not be once named among you, as becometh saints." (Eph. 5:3) There are certain things that shouldn't even be uttered by people without God totally convicting them in their lie. I backslid in fornication a couple of times in my walk, but God! He is a deliverer and will set you on course. You must want it!

That conviction is something serious. You're in danger if you no longer become convicted when you know God and your life aren't in alignment. Paul discussed mourning those who are fallen and it says, "And lest, when I come again, my God will humble me among you, and that I shall bewail many which have sinned already, and have not repented of the uncleanness and fornication and lasciviousness which they have committed." (2 Cor. 12:21) God offers a way of escape when you submit to Him. He tells us to resist the devil and he will flee (Jas. 4:7). Resisting today can be as simple as blocking from calling and social media, unfollowing certain people, staying away from certain places, and ceasing from watching certain things. Minding your gates! Resist and go with God.

Prayer

Forgive me, Lord, for attaching to the god Baal. I renounce his power in my life, my loins, and all my members. Leave from me, Baal, in the name of Jesus! Father, purge me with hyssop, and I shall be clean: wash me, and I shall be whiter than snow. I denounce and throw down the spirit of fornication, adultery, and wickedness in high places. I bind you in Jesus' name and cast you into the abyss. You have no power! You have no rights! I take legal authority of my body, mind, and soul in the name of Jesus. I hand that authority to Yahweh! I decree that this body is the temple of the Holy Ghost! Remove every blemish, stain, or residue of sins of my past right now, in Jesus' name. Amen!

EXPERIENCE 9: PRIDE

Such a small word, but one that packs a deadly cocktail. Pride can have you so high on self-elevation that you can't see the destruction you cause. Your main concern is keeping yourself straight with material things and external beauty. All the while you're unfulfilled and hollow in your soul. "(For if a man know not how to rule his own house, how shall he take care of the church of God?) Not a novice, lest being lifted up with pride he fall into the condemnation of the devil." (1Tim. 3:5-6)

Factor in one thing in this scripture. You. Are. The. Church.

> Know ye not that ye are the temple of God, and that the Spirit of God dwelleth in you? If any man defile the temple of God, him shall God destroy; for the temple of God is holy, which temple ye are. (1 Cor. 3:16-17)

Elevating yourself higher than The Creator is a dangerous thing. It also makes you unaware of self. It makes you unteachable and unusable and causes a breach between you and the Father. If you and God are separated, then naturally you're outside of Christ as well. They are one in the same.

This is how people get to heaven and end up judged and sentenced to damnation. They accept the call of Jesus and didn't cultivate the relationship in order to maintain salvation. They don't keep His commandments. Accepting the call of Christ is step one. Working to change sinful ways daily is what gets you a mansion in heaven with your name on the mailbox. The race is for those who endure to the end… who stay with God to the end.

I'm not saying you will be perfect out the gate. God's grace is sufficient for you as you go through the process of purging. While Jesus works the world out of you, God is shining you up and directing you in His way.

There is something about giving up your will and ways for God's will and way for your life. Do you think I knew when I was a teen that I would be writing a book of deliverance for you? I was going to travel the world; live how I want, and do what I want. I can still travel, but it's so much better now that I have the peace of God! Living in your purpose is a high but if you have your mind set on things and your own agenda then you will miss the mark. You will miss God's blessing and a life fulfilled. It's hard to say that you don't know what's best for you. It's hard to say you don't know what you need.

If you allow God in and give Him space to operate how He desires, He will have you in unexpected places and living in bliss. "The pride of thine heart hath deceived thee, thou that dwellest in clefts of the rock, whose habitation is high; that saith in his heart, Who shall bring me down to the ground?" (Obad. 1:3) You're in your high-rise making the most money you have ever made, taking the most from people that you have ever taken, and walking with your nose so far in the air and feeling untouchable. Then the prophet Obadiah says, "Though thou exalt thyself as the eagle, and though thou set thy nest among the stars, thence will I bring thee down, saith the Lord." (Obad. 1:4)

God has a way of checking His children. It's up to you how hard the lesson is on you. When you can discern yourself and yield to the Holy Spirit, you pass certain pitfalls. Life will bring you sorrows just living. People die, jobs close, and accidents happen, but when it's internal and self-inflicted that's another situation. As God cleans you up, don't think it was by your own strength. As God elevates you, don't think it's through your knowledge and experience. Yes, the things you have learned in life help you maintain, but the favor of the Lord is what makes you a cornerstone. "Pride goeth before destruction, and an haughty spirit before a fall." (Prov. 16:18)

The Lord will set you up on high places when your heart is right and fixed on Him. When we allow pride to creep in, that's when our fall is great. There are some people who are so full of pride and they seem to get promotion on top of promotion. God had to tell me not to get upset at what looks like success because the higher a person is elevated, the harder the impact when they fall.

Don't get so detached from Jesus the Deliverer that you can't see your error. Don't start to judge those who are wobbling in Christ and learning how to walk. Remember the beginnings and be humble. Walk in humility. God showed the ultimate display of love when He gave Jesus to us undeserved. Have that same compassion for others as you go through life. "When pride cometh, then cometh shame: but with the lowly is wisdom." (Prov. 11:2) There are times you can think you're on your "A" game and unstoppable. There are people you put down along the way and whose life you made miserable. Those same people you will have to approach with a look of shame when it's time to repent.

I'm so thankful for Facebook, because it allowed me to quickly repent to those I offended over the years when I wasn't saved. God would bring up that person to me and what I did, and I had to confess the evil and repent. He has no desire for there to be anything someone can hold over you – not even you against yourself! If they choose not to accept repentance, that's not on you. You're working your salvation for your reward, not theirs. You must release who you were and pray God removes the scales from your eyes so that you may see you how He sees you.

"The wicked, through the pride of his countenance, will not seek after God: God is not in all his thoughts." (Psa. 10:4)

Allow God to have His complete work. Be open to the change that will take place in your life. Friends, geography, finances, family, and occupations may change when you get on course with your destiny in Jesus. We received examples when God called the 12 disciples. They were working and scheming; minding their own business when they received the call. Like you! Minding your own business, doing what you do and you heard Jesus call you. That pull at your heart when it was time for salvation, that was the call you answered. Continue in Christ and allow Him to clean you up. Stay in the Word, get in a church that is teaching sound doctrine. The leader in that church must be teaching the Word of God unapologetically and following it accordingly. "How do I know they are doing that, Ilaya?" you may ask. You will know because you have sought the Lord and read it for yourself. The Lord gives us a spirit of discernment and we must try the spirit by the spirit to see if it is of

God (1 John 4:1).

Prayer

Great God Jehovah who is higher than I, be high and lifted. I repent for operating in the pride of life. Forgive me for thinking of myself higher than the ant and the sparrow. Forgive me for putting my trust in myself, money, and other material things and not totally surrendering to You. Forgive me for being high-minded and haughty in my thinking and looking down on others in distress. Forgive me for not having compassion for my brothers and sisters in this world. You asked when You were hungry, did I feed You and when You thirsted, did I give You drink? I understand when I help those in need I in turn glorify You. Thank You for giving me a heart of flesh and given me a quickened spirit of repentance. Help me to turn and continually see the error of my ways so that I may stay on the spiritual course of destiny with You. In Jesus Christ's name I pray. Amen!

EXPERIENCE 10: LACK OF NATURAL AFFECTION

Personality traits have everything to do with whether a person is Type A, B, and so on. When you can't operate in the flow of affection naturally then that is different. If your initial response isn't to shake a person's hand when they extend it in greeting, that is a "you" problem. You may be a germaphobe, but most places have running water, soap, and hand sanitizer. You have a spirit of fear. You may regret shaking that person's hand, but you do it.

Goodness, don't get asked to hug a person! People act like someone unleashed the plagues of Egypt. You start thinking too highly of yourself, wondering if the person has lice or fleas or if he or she smells. There was a person at the church I went to who gave a testimony. It was really a confession! It was the part of the service where we were led to fellowship. The pastor asked us to hug a person and make sure it's not a person we knew. The person on the confessional block said she heard the Lord as clear as day say go give a specific person a hug. She refused! The confession continued with her saying how she preconceived that the person she was to hug smelled and didn't want that scent rubbing off on her. Plus, she said she wasn't a hugger anyway.

When you lack natural affection, there are walls within you that reject embrace. This rejection comes across in the natural, but it also blocks you spiritually from the embrace of Jesus and your Heavenly Father. It hurts to touch tender spots, but you must examine the wound so that you can know how to treat it! Loneliness, rejection, feeling like the outsider, being untrusting, and feeling hurt can beat you down until you no longer can embrace your children, family, and even yourself.

When we have this divide, we often use sex to fill the void. It's a temporary fix because after the act, we still feel void and alone. It's like if a person gets too close, they will see what we try to hide. "Set your affection on things above, not on things on the earth." (Col. 3:2) It's when we don't look straight ahead but backwards at our past that we get thrown off-course. We self-medicate in order not to feel, but we build walls in order to keep the hurt out, not knowing we are holding the pain of the past in and holding captive our ability to be free.

God didn't call us to be shut off from the world. I spend most of my days behind a computer but I make an effort to go out, see friends, and attend church because the Word says,

> And let us consider one another to provoke unto love and to good works: Not forsaking the assembling of ourselves together, as the manner of some is; but exhorting one another: and so much the more, as ye see the day approaching. (Heb. 10:24-25)

People will try to give a pass to those who have mental challenges, but that's the stumbling block. You weren't born without affection. You yearned for your mother's breast, her smell, and the warmth of her body. That is instinct! Babies scoot out the gate. I remember my daughter was asleep on our king-size bed and one month old. She was about six inches from me and sleeping. I fell asleep also. We were the only ones home. When I woke up, she was right under me, snuggled and still asleep.

It's about survival! We need people. We need each other to be encouraged, to stay on course in Christ, and to convict each other of wrongdoing. Along with the prayer, your task is to hug someone today. It will be uncomfortable at first, especially if you don't consider yourself a hugger, but once you start allowing your walls to fall you will receive freedom. Deliverance comes by wanting it and by your actions. What God tells you is key to your deliverance, especially in that moment. Do you accept the challenge?

Prayer

Father, I pray the walls around my heart come down just as the walls of Jericho. Remove every hurt. Remove every memory of the hurt, even the sting of it in the name of Jesus. Make me free, Father, to receive love. Make me free so that I can be compassionate to others. Give me a heart of flesh to receive an honest embrace of sincerity. Lord, allow me to be open to new friendships. Remove from me the old nature of using sex to fill the void of feeling alone. Remove my protective devices that have failed me over and over. Change me and make me new. In Jesus Christ's name. Amen!

EXPERIENCE 11: ADDICTIONS

I'm pretty sure Addiction has hit every family, in every generation, and has hurt several people. It is seen as an illness, but the reality is that it's a spirit. It flows with neglect, low self-worth, all abuse, and regret. It falls into the posse of Lust because sex can be just as addictive as weed, shooting up, and drinking in excess.

There were times when I couldn't help but masturbate or have sex. It was pressing. There was a need to release. I felt as if I would burst open if I didn't. I mean, I went seven of the ten years of celibacy not even masturbating. Whoa! I know, right? It wasn't until I got too close to that man, in my backsliding, that my old ways came right back like I never quit.

That's what addiction does. It hugs you like you never left, like you're the long-lost relative who returned home, and it still has a chair in your favorite spot. The same people may even be there! Titus 2:11-12 reads, "For the grace of God that bringeth salvation hath appeared to all men, Teaching us that, denying ungodliness and worldly lusts, we should live soberly, righteously, and godly, in this present world"; all we need to do is deny it.

The word 'no' is so powerful! When you use 'no' to some people they get upset. Inconveniencing you so that they are not inconvenienced is the dance of life. When you get in the habit of saying "no" to what doesn't agree with your spirit, you don't have the time, you don't want to backslide, and you're trying your hardest to live right. Don't get me wrong – it's going to take multiple "no's" to get your peace.

The best example is the temptation of Christ in Matthew 4. Yes! Homework. If you've ever been to a church, you've probably heard it preached, but get it in your spirit. Read it and read it over and over. In summary, the Lord Jesus was hungry because He fasted 40 days and He was human. The devil promised Him everything a person with a yearning in their flesh would want. Each time, Jesus denied the devil's advances and Jesus did so with scripture. Jesus is the Word of God. If the Word of God had to take the Word of God to fight the devil, then what do you think you will need to fight the seduction of the devil? You got it! You need the Word of God.

> For we have not an high priest which cannot be touched with the feeling of our infirmities: but was in all points tempted like as we are, yet without sin. Let us therefore come boldly unto the throne of grace, that we may obtain mercy, and find grace to help in time of need. (Heb. 4:15-16)

He suffered also, and is the example we have in order to make it through this life.

"And call upon me in the day of trouble: I will deliver thee, and thou shalt glorify me." (Psa. 50:15) God's Word will not go unanswered and neither are you when you ask of Him to help you to stay close to Him. God's desire is not for any of His children to stray. He had the Law of Moses and found it less effective than sacrificing Himself — His Son — for you to choose Him.

There are certain friends who come with addiction. Stay away from those people. Stay away from those places! My father was on crack for 20 years. Even know that he has been 15 years sober, he can know where to find the drugs in a brand-new city. He must consistently resist the devil. I know I must be his crutch when he is going through hard times, because it's easy to fall into addiction patterns when you are feeling the way you did when you were deep in your addiction. You need an accountability partner to help you maintain deliverance.

Another example is my friend's mother. She got saved and that very day of salvation, the people of God prayed for her and she received Christ and those spirits left her. She would go into strip clubs, whore houses, and crack houses with the Word of God in hand and did not fall into the trap. If you're not strong like my friend's mom, then this scripture is for you: "Be not deceived: evil communications corrupt good manners." (1 Cor. 15:33) Bad company can undo good habits faster than your reciting the prayer to receive your salvation. *If you received it reading this book, know the angels are dancing and praising in heaven that you have returned!*

"Submit yourselves therefore to God. Resist the devil, and he will flee from you." (Jas. 4:7) Tell him "NO!" Fight the devil with the weapon he could never defeat: the Word of God! It is imperative to your deliverance that you read the Bible. I can't stress that enough. Take no breaks, vacations, sick leave, maternity leave, sabbaticals, or any other time off you can think of, because that could be the day you stumble. When the demons get into your house once it's clean, they bring the posse with them that makes you worse than your original state before Christ.

> And not only so, but we glory in tribulations also: knowing that tribulation worketh patience; And patience, experience; and experience, hope: And hope maketh not ashamed; because the love of God is shed abroad in our hearts by the Holy Ghost which is given unto us." (Rom. 5:3-5)

Count it an honor and privilege that the enemy wants you back. If you're not tempted by the enemy, then he may have you in his grips, and you're operating for him. Continue to have your heart fixed toward the Love of God, the Word of God, and the Son Jesus Christ. The comforter, the Holy Spirit will be your blanket and teacher and bring the knowledge of God back to your remembrance until the end of your days. You've been made new! Believe it continually.

Stay woke! Not in a way that you know your heritage and the manipulation of man, but stay awake in your walk with Christ! I backslid. I did it of my own accord. I made up my mind, heart, and spirit that I was tired of waiting. Once you're tempted — *and you will be* — as you walk with the Lord remember this scripture, "Watch and pray, that ye enter not into temptation: the spirit indeed is willing, but the flesh is weak." (Matt. 26:41) You will see the devil has no new tricks. You will be like a sharpshooter when seeing his advances, and you will be equipped with the Word of God and win every battle when you go in the strength of Christ. Resist the devil. Tell him "NO!" Keep telling him you're not having it. Strive for holiness and fight hard to maintain your deliverance!

Prayer

Father, remove the taste of my addiction. Remove its fragrance, its sound, and even the emotions that trigger me to find comfort in addiction. Lord, I pray that You be all that I need. You be my yearning desire. You be my husband man, my bridegroom, and my deliverer from all manner of addiction. Give me the strength to resist the devil. Give me the boldness and the fire to say 'no' continually. Make Your wants for my life my wants. Place in me holiness. Sanctify my mind, heart, and soul. Make me to see You in my reflection. Set hot coals to my feet when I desire those unclean places, unclean acts, and unclean companions in the name of Jesus. Be a lamp to my feet and guide me through the gospel. Teach me to fight using Your words. Place people in my life that mean me good and not harm. Sharpen my discernment so that I can see the enemy from afar. Clear my eyesight so that I can see there is more that are for me than against me. In Jesus Christ's name. Amen!

AFTERWORD

Deliverance is for those who ask. Saved or unsaved, there is an unction of the Spirit of God that lets you know there is an imbalance. He lets you know that you and the Spirit are not on one accord. It's up to you to fix it and get it right! You can be saved, Holy Ghost-filled, and a Bible thumper and still need deliverance. There shouldn't be shame regarding the matter, but a religious spirit only abounds when you're not free. Some organized religions make it seem like accepting Christ is the only thing needed and then demons can't touch you. If you have demons dwelling within going into it and you don't take authority and get them out of you, then they will lay dormant until the perfect time to rise up. Do not be ignorant of the devil's devices!

Things can get messy! There may be vomit, snot, and tears. Have a towel ready. Make sure there is water and Gatorade stocked to replenish your body. Make time for rest. Self-deliverance is possible. That is what you've done with the help of this book. There may be voices that are audible. Do not be alarmed! Ask their name and call them out.

Seek God and continually seek Him in the Word of God. If you fall, repent quickly and turn from it. There will be things that continually arise that you must address, but know that God is an everlasting arm that you can lean on. Know that your salvation is sure. Share it! Share your love for Christ with others. Don't hide your light under a lampshade because of your past. It's just that – your past. It's behind you!

Pray daily! It is imperative you're filled with the Holy Spirit and have the evidence of speaking in tongues as soon as possible if you haven't already. Christ left us this precious gift because He knew help is still needed. Pray in your heavenly language daily. Pray the scripture daily over yourself, people in your house, and your life.

Get in a church that feeds your soul. Ask God what gift is in you that He is holding you responsible for. Get around like-minded believers who have the drive to press on and learn their purpose as well. Allow the Holy Spirit to lead your steps and choose your friendships wisely and with discernment. Nothing is too hard for God so when it gets rough for you, allow Him to take over. Embrace the change that is coming. Embrace the peace. Embrace the Love of Christ.

Love God. Love Others. Love Self.

ABOUT THE AUTHOR

Ilaya Brown accepted her call into the Ministry March of 2019. She said God was bugging her like a fly at a barbeque. Her calling has been something she tried to ignore and she did so successfully for a decade, or so she thought! She often found herself at church, hosting prayer groups, and just trying to uplift those who were seeking to do better in life.

Ilaya is the writer of the ***Turn That Floozy Series*** and has been a published author for nine years. Having pledged her complete obedience to God, she found herself taking a break from writing Christian fiction and instead completing her first 'God help' work. She has a Bachelor's Degree in Small Business Management and an Associate's Degree in Fashion Marketing. Fashion has been a love of hers, along with writing. Her online boutique — 'And Amazed' — sells women's clothing.

Her greatest joy — whom she gets to nurture and watch grow — is her daughter, who shares her love of reading. Ilaya's passion is seeing souls come to Christ, the saved receiving the in-filling of the Holy Spirit, and saints getting delivered.

Made in the USA
Columbia, SC
15 March 2021

34265943R00067